St. Louis
YESTERDAY & TODAY ™

Betty Burnett

WEST
SIDE
PUBLISHING

Betty Burnett is a St. Louisan by choice, a Connecticut Yankee by birth. As a historian, she's written on a variety of topics. Her book about the Delta Force won an ALA-VOYA award in 2002. She holds a Ph.D. in American Studies from Saint Louis University.

Scott Avetta has been published in many books and magazines. His artwork can be seen in and around St. Louis, from BJC Hospitals to Washington University. Avetta teaches photography and offers workshops at various locations. More information on his work can be found at www.scottavetta.com.

Lew Portnoy has had 2,500-plus assignments in sports journalism and location photography and has won many regional and national awards. After becoming the photographer for the St. Louis Blues Hockey Club in 1968, Portnoy has photographed nearly every major sporting event in North America. More information and photographs are available at www.lewportnoy.com.

Facts verified by Adam T. Michalski.

Special thanks to the Mercantile Library, Missouri Historical Society, St. Louis Archdiocese Archives, St. Louis Public Library, and the Western Historical Manuscript Collection. Thanks also to Amy Woods Butler for her help and support with the research.

Considered the gateway to the West, the Arch represents the spirit of St. Louis. Visitors can take a tram ride 630 feet up to the observation platform for a bird's-eye view of the city.

Contents

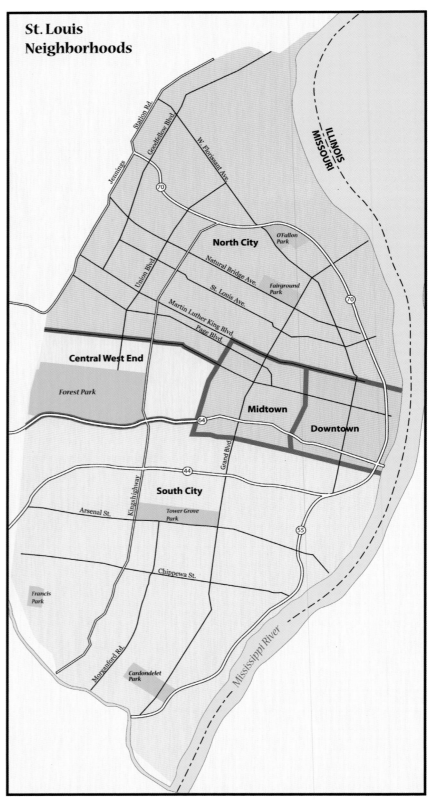

St. Louis
Neighborhoods

Above: This drawing of Monk's Mound in Cahokia, Illinois, shows it as it was in the mid-19th century. Cahokia Mounds State Park reconstructed the hills that the Hopewell people originally built in the St. Louis area. As many as 20 smaller mounds once stood north of Laclede's Landing in St. Louis.

Right: The history and character of the city of St. Louis can be found in each of its unique neighborhoods. This map shows the prominent districts of the city today, along with some of the major streets and parks.

One of the Finest Cities

The bluffs along the Mississippi River just south of the Missouri River seemed deserted when Pierre Laclede and Auguste Chouteau arrived in 1764 to establish an outpost dedicated to King Louis IX. The Hopewell people lived in the area beginning around 500 B.C.E., disappearing about A.D. 400. They left large earthen mounds, seemingly built with knowledge of astronomy. Although most of these mounds were destroyed by land developers, many can still be seen across the Mississippi River in Cahokia Mounds State Park, where the Hopewell society has been reconstructed.

The Hopewells were farmers and traders who exchanged goods with other Native nations throughout the continent. The first European St. Louisans were also traders. Pierre Laclede was a business-man, not an explorer. He hoped to build a multimillion-dollar fur business similar to his first outpost (a small settlement in upper Louisiana) with the Osage.

Laclede came to New Orleans from his native France in 1755 as a young man seeking his fortune. There he fell in love with Marie Therese Chouteau, a young wife and mother who had been abandoned by her husband. The pair could not marry because divorce was not permitted in Catholic society, despite the fact that Madame Chouteau's husband was no longer in America. They decided to live together as common-law partners, and their four children were baptized as Chouteaus, not Lacledes. Laclede also accepted the role of father to his step-son, Auguste Chouteau, who became his right-hand man and continued the fur trade, enriching his family considerably.

FRENCH CULTURE

Laclede is credited with being the founder of St. Louis. He is reported to have said, "I have found a site on which to form my settlement which might hereafter become one of the finest cities in America." However, it was Madame Chouteau who provided the social atmosphere that attracted French settlers from both sides of the river. She followed Laclede upriver several months after he raised the French flag in St. Louis—she wanted to wait until after the birth of her fifth child. She made the long journey north in a flatboat with a five-year-old, a three-year-old, a one-year-old, and an infant. After that experience, a settled life in a spacious St. Louis home was surely appreciated.

Life Along the Mississippi

A painting by Henry Lewis shows what the St. Louis riverfront was like in 1846 *(left)*. Three years later, a fire devastated the riverfront and almost destroyed the city. In the 20th century, the McDonald's Riverboat was advertised as the only floating McDonald's in the world *(below)*. Originating in the 1980s, it had an ice cream stand and a souvenir shop. It was a fixture on the St. Louis riverfront until it closed in the 1990s. Also shown below, the Poplar Street Bridge spans the Mississippi River, carrying approximately 120,000 cars and trucks in both directions on interstates 55, 64, and 70. Opened in 1967, the bridge was officially named for Bernard F. Dickmann, the mayor who pulled the city out of the Great Depression. Its eastern end crosses the area once known as Bloody Island, the 19th-century dueling ground.

Pierre Laclede died in 1778. He did not live to see his village Americanized, or his children established. However, all the Chouteau children and grandchildren eventually prospered and married well, bringing Papins, Gratiots, Labbadies, and Cerres into the expanding family. By 1809, when St. Louis was incorporated as a town, the French culture was in decline. Now, it is hard to find French influence beyond street signs and the fleur-de-lis of St. Louis University. (St. Genevieve to the south and Florissant to the north have preserved much of their French heritage.)

SHARING A CITY

If a time-lapse camera captured the movement of St. Louisans from 1809 forward, it would show people fanning out in all directions as they established neighborhoods and towns. Then they moved on, while others moved in to take their places: Yankees, African Americans, Southerners, Germans, Irish, Italians, Bosnians, Hispanics, and Asians. Rail tracks and highways followed them, giving them access to the city's core, as well as taking them farther afield.

In 2003, the riverfront was busy with barge traffic and riverboats. Today, only the *Admiral* riverboat, which houses the President Casino, remains. Plans are underway for a revitalization of the area.

Like many other cities, St. Louis today is fragmented not only by highways and suburban boundaries, but also by income, education, language, cultural background, religion, and generation. At the same time, its residents are unified by the need to work and provide for their families, educate their children, and enjoy the environment. St. Louis residents have experienced, together, the long-term results of racial segregation, a distinc-tive blues style, ten World Series cham-pionships, river-valley humidity, belly bombers, strikes, the closing of factories, Lucky Lindy, the birth of the League of Women Voters, riverboat gambling, and Buster Brown. St. Louisians share a history. And this history can be seen in the city of St. Louis's profound sense of spirit that is encapsulated in the symbol of the Arch, the gateway to the West.

Ashes to the Arch

When Pierre Laclede laid out his town in 1764, he set aside land for government, the church, and the people, as well as for his trading post. This pattern is seen in downtown St. Louis today, with its acres of green space, numerous church spires, and handsome government buildings. Along the three streets of Laclede's town were 75 buildings, mainly private homes that doubled as small businesses: candlemakers, blacksmiths, seamstresses, and greengrocers. In 1766, the entire town of St. Louis—population 300—could fit on today's Arch grounds.

The town grew slowly over the next 40 years. Although it was under Spanish rule for 36 of those years, it remained solidly French until 1804, when settlers began moving to their new Louisiana Territory to take up residence. The fur trade was Missouri's Gold Rush. Yankee traders and would-be mountain men streamed into St. Louis, hoping to make a quick profit on beaver pelts and buffalo hides. Soon after, outfitters and general stores were established.

In 1817, the steamboat *Zebulon Pike* docked in St. Louis, and almost overnight the city became a seaport of sorts. Market and Morgan streets were graded to meet the levee, and by 1840, as many as 150 steamboats were loading and unloading on a single day. The Mississippi connected St. Louis to eastern cities through Cincinnati and Pittsburgh and to New York and Europe through New Orleans. Cotton and tobacco were processed here before being shipped. In the 1840s, the population exploded with a growth rate of 373 percent. This was also the decade that the Oregon, California, and Mormon trails were blazed. All these western settlers bought St. Louis-made goods to take with them. Hawken rifles and Murphy wagons were produced in downtown St. Louis, as well as ropes, chains, wagon wheels, woodenware, and hundreds of hardware items.

The Santa Fe Trail, which originated in mid-Missouri, opened up trade with Mexico in 1821, the same year that Missouri became a state. As much as $100,000 in Mexican silver came to Missouri from Santa Fe traders each year. Much of this money found its way to St. Louis, giving the city capital for investments.

DISASTER STRIKES

In 1849, the steamboat *White Cloud*, moored at a city dock, caught fire. As was the custom, the boat was cut loose

The *Golden Eagle* ferried passengers along the Chain of Rocks Canal in the 20th century.

with the hope it would burn itself out. Instead, winds pushed it into boat after boat as it drifted downstream. Twenty-three boats caught fire, and the wind carried sparks to the cargo stacked on Wharf Street. From there the fire spread to the city. Volunteer firefighters used gunpowder to create a firebreak, and eventually the fire was extinguished. About 400 buildings and 15 city blocks were destroyed; the property loss was put at $6.1 million. The disaster spurred the development of a professional fire department and the use of brick construction in the rebuilding of the city.

CHANGING WITH THE TIMES

The city experienced a substantial dip in trade revenues during the Civil War, when commerce with the South was halted and river traffic was primarily military. After the Civil War, railroads replaced steamboats to move freight. To compete in this market, St. Louis needed a way across the Mississippi. The construction of a bridge began in 1867, designed by engineer James B. Eads (the inventor of the diving bell), but there were numerous problems with building such a new-fangled structure, including a tornado that tore through the area in 1871. The bridge was not open for traffic until 1874.

Retail trade grew as the city prospered. Scruggs, Vandervoort & Barney Dry Goods Company became one of the largest retail firms in the nation, offering products as well as hosting public events. David May opened his first store in 1905; it would eventually become Famous-Barr. William Danforth, another shrewd salesman, developed Ralston-Purina into a worldwide animal feed supplier because "horses always have to eat."

DOWNTOWN

Throughout the 19th century, downtown was home to several ethnic groups. As waves of immigrants arrived, some residents moved west to escape the city's air pollution, inadequate sewer system, and crime.

In order to spruce up the downtown waterfront, Luther Ely Smith, lawyer and St. Louis promoter, proposed a memorial for Meriwether Lewis and William Clark (members of the 1800s Corps of Discovery expedition). He convinced Mayor Bernard

Dickman and Congress to agree to the project. A 90-acre site was cleared by May 1942. Delay followed delay, and the Jefferson National Expansion Memorial was not completed until 1965.

Since 1980, downtown planners have tried new ideas to attract businesses while watching corporate headquarters move away. Landmarks Association was formed to try to preserve/restore old buildings and find new uses for them.

Downtown is the one place in the metro area that belongs to everyone, whether or not they work and live there. It's where county residents bring visitors to enjoy the riverfront; where football, baseball, and ice hockey are played; and where parades march in celebration. The founders of this busy city, Pierre Laclede and Madame Chouteau, would be proud.

Eads Bridge

The downtown St. Louis riverfront, circa 2003. In 1766, the entire town could have fit on the Arch grounds.

RIVERFRONT

The St. Louis riverfront stretches from the Chain of Rocks Bridge in the north to Jefferson Barracks Bridge in the south, yet for most people "the riverfront" means the Arch grounds. The city's riverfront was its commercial and industrial hub for more than 150 years. It's only relatively recently that residents began thinking about beautifying the riverfront and using it for recreation. Meanwhile, old manufacturing facilities and warehouses, once dependent on the river, stand vacant both north and south of downtown.

Robert E. Lee, before he became a Civil War general, was an army engineer—the first to tackle the Mississippi river in this area. From 1837 to 1839, he supervised the building of underwater dikes made of alternating layers of stones and brush in an attempt to force the river to circumvent the sandbars that grew into islands. Bloody Island was the most notorious—being neither in Missouri nor Illinois, it was considered no man's land where duels could be fought without penalty. (Bloody Island was eventually joined to the shore in East St. Louis.) Lee's dikes did not hold for very long, and soon the U.S. Army Corps of Engineers was working full time on canalizing, damming, and locking the river. During the 1993 flood, which reached 49½ feet above flood stage, the highest in the city's history, the 52-foot floodwall kept the rushing, burbling, chemical-rich flood water from overtaking the city.

Top: The St. Louis riverfront was a busy place in 1907. *Bottom:* "Hoovervilles," named for President Herbert Hoover because of his hands-off economic policy, popped up along the riverfront during the Great Depression of the 1930s, when foreclosures forced people out of their homes.

In the 1800s, the luxurious *Grand Republic* was one of hundreds of steamboats that stopped in St. Louis.

RIVERBOATS

Buying a steamboat in the 1840s was a high-risk investment, but if it paid off, the profits could be phenomenal. Boiler explosions and underwater snags were the two biggest dangers, and ordinary wear and tear gave an average steamboat a life expectancy of less than three years. Still, during the years before the railroad took freight traffic away from the river, steamboats were the best way to move goods and people. Scores of paddle wheelers, stern-wheelers, and packets lined the city docks on any given day, waiting to be loaded and unloaded. Some boats brought cholera with them. The worst epidemic arrived in the summer of 1849, when one-tenth of the city's population died of the disease, including 91-year-old Pierre Chouteau, son of Pierre Laclede and Marie Therese Chouteau.

Floating palaces or showboats brought entertainers and melodrama to dozens of small towns along the river. The *Goldenrod*, a stern-wheeler built in 1909, was reputedly the largest, most elaborately decorated showboat ever constructed. After traveling the river for almost 30 years piloted by Captain Bill Menke, it was docked at the Locust Street landing where it continued to present popular melodrama for many years. The musical *Showboat* was based on the adventures of the *Goldenrod*. With the invention of motion pictures, the popularity of showboats waned. Today, moored casinos have replaced the venerable riverboats.

Barge traffic has also played a significant role in the economy of the Midwest. It's estimated that over 90 percent of corn and soybeans exported from the Gulf are transported by barge on the Mississippi River.

Barges are some of the cheapest and cleanest forms of transportation; barge traffic is heavy on the Mississippi.

THE ARCH

In the 1930s and 1940s, St. Louisan Luther Ely Smith advocated commemorating the westward migration of the 19th century pioneers and the expedition of Lewis and Clark with some sort of riverfront park. Eventually he got backing from Congress. Other national memorials were designed as a straight vertical line (Washington Monument), a cube (Lincoln Memorial), or a globe (Jefferson Memorial). Eero Saarinen, the architect chosen to design the Jefferson Expansion National Memorial, used an arch. He figured that a weighted catenary curve should last 1,000 years. Although the design won the 1947–1948 competition, excavation didn't begin until April 1961. In February 1963, the first aboveground section appeared, and the Arch was topped off on October 28, 1965.

At 630 feet tall (and 630 feet wide), the Arch is twice as tall as the Statue of Liberty, 150 feet taller than the pyramids, and 350 feet shorter than the Eiffel Tower. Each leg is made up of double-walled, equilateral triangle sections. The walls of each section are connected by high-strength steel rods, making it a self-supporting, stressed-skin structure, theoretically able to withstand anything Mother Nature might throw at it.

The Arch has become the instantly recognizable symbol of St. Louis and, with the underground Museum of Westward Expansion, is a major tourist attraction.

Above: Watching the Arch go up was a favorite spectator sport during the 1960s. *Right:* Fur trader Manuel Lisa, one-time partner of Pierre Chouteau and William Clark, built this rubble-stone warehouse on the riverfront in 1818. By the late 19th century, the building, with mansard roof added, was called the Old Rock House and held a saloon that drew jazz musicians from Memphis and New Orleans. To make way for the Arch grounds, the building was dismantled. Some of its stones are on display in the museum at the Old Courthouse.

Old Courthouse

Two nationally significant trials were held in the Old Courthouse, which is now part of the Jefferson National Historic Memorial. Slaves Dred and Harriet Scott sued for their freedom in 1846. After trials and retrials with conflicting results, a jury decided they should be free, but their owner appealed to the Missouri Supreme Court, which ruled in the owner's favor. This decision went to the U.S. Supreme Court, which declared in 1857 that slaves are not citizens and thus do not have the right to sue. In 1872, Virginia Minor tried to register to vote, citing the 14th Amendment. When she was not allowed, her husband sued (she didn't even have the right to sue). The court ruled that although women were citizens, they could not vote.

Right: The Arch and the riverfront provide a nice backdrop for the Old Cathedral.

GOVERNMENT

The city's first mayor, William Carr Lane, was elected in 1823. Fortunately for the city, he organized the infrastructure as well as a public health system. The city grew, as did the bureaucracy.

In 1904, a new City Hall was built in the French château style to reflect the city's French heritage. Much earlier, the aldermen had renamed streets, changing the French *rues* to a more prosaic system: tree streets running east and west and numbered streets running north and south. The first mayor to serve in this new City Hall was reformer Rolla Wells, who called for a "new St. Louis." He was responsible for a clean water system (the previous cloudy, bacteria-laden water led to myriad illnesses), landscaped parks, and the establishment of public baths, all in preparation for the 1904 World's Fair. Other memorable mayors were bricklayer Henry Kiel, who oversaw the enactment of the City Charter of 1914 that organized the city into 28 wards; real estate entrepreneur Bernard Dickmann, who made the air breathable in winter by ending the use of soft coal and shepherded the development of the Jefferson Memorial; and engineer Ray Tucker, who instituted the City Earnings Tax and began an aggressive urban renewal program.

Above: Four St. Louis landmarks line up on Market Street looking east: Union Station, the Civil Courts Building, the Old Courthouse, and the Arch. *Left:* Peeking out from behind the left-hand side of City Hall is the Thomas Eagleton Federal Courthouse.

Old Post Office

Construction on the Old Post Office and Custom House *(above)* took ten years and nearly $6 million. It was built like a fortress with a 28-foot-deep moat and sliding iron shutters. Although the Civil War had ended years earlier, fears of rebellion and mob violence remained. The building was almost demolished in the 1980s, but the efforts of Landmarks Association kept it alive; it has been handsomely refurbished.

Above right: The aldermanic chambers are quiet on a day of rest in City Hall in the late 1930s. *Right:* St. Louisans line up in the Civil Courts Building in May 1944 to get ration books. During World War II, gasoline, meat, dairy products, and shoes were rationed.

RETAIL

The first retail stores downtown catered to people who were leaving the area—fur traders and western settlers—offering such items as harnesses, boots, nails, and bolts of cloth. Once ready-made clothes became available after the Civil War, shopping became an art, and the garment district along Washington Avenue blossomed. Almost everything wearable was made in downtown St. Louis: hats, coats, suits, dresses, and shoes. The Famous Co. opened in 1873, attracting homemakers to the store with housewares as well as clothing. In 1892, the May Co. of Cleveland bought the company; in 1911, it bought the Barr Co., creating Famous-Barr, a stylish five-story department store. Scruggs, Vandervoort & Barney and Stix, Baer & Fuller provided competition. These large stores offered middle-class women an array of fine clothing and household items, comfortable lounges, private changing rooms, beauty salons, and tearooms. During World War II, downtown stores began staying open at night to accommodate shift workers, and the streets were alive with shoppers. At holiday time, the stores' lavish decorations brought families downtown to admire the store windows as part of their Christmas traditions. As late as 1959, shopping downtown for women meant dressing up and wearing high heels, gloves, and hats.

All three department stores have since disappeared from downtown. Macy's now operates in the Famous-Barr building. Suburban malls and large discount stores changed shopping habits beginning in the 1960s, and downtown is no longer a retail mecca.

Left: Woolworth's, 1914. *Above:* A fixture in St. Louis, the May Co. was bought out in 2005, changing the downtown Famous-Barr into Macy's.

In May 1944, toward the end of World War II, a uniformed black sailor walked into Woolworth's downtown to get lunch; he was denied service. The Citizens Civil Rights Committee responded by sending blacks and whites to the lunch counter at Katz Drugstore, and the summer of sit-ins began. It would be 20 more years before open accommodations became the law of the land.

In the days when a one-income family was the norm, women could spend hours shopping downtown and have a relaxed lunch in a tearoom. This 1959 photo was taken at Stix, Baer & Fuller, one of St. Louis's premier department stores. Founded in 1892, Stix disappeared when Dillards bought it in 1983.

MEDIA

Since the first *Gazette* was printed in 1808, dozens of newspapers have appeared, changed, merged, and disappeared—the *Star-Times* and *Globe-Democrat* are among the vanished. Hungarian immigrant Joseph Pulitzer bought two small newspapers, *The Post* and *The Dispatch,* in the 1870s, merged them, and imbued the new *Post-Dispatch* with a taste for investigative journalism and advocacy for the concerns of ordinary citizens. After the Pulitzer family sold the *St. Louis Post-Dispatch* in 2005 to the out-of-town Lee Enterprises, the paper changed its emphasis to infotainment.

Three African American newspapers are published in the city, the *Argus* (beginning in 1912), *The American* (from 1928), and *The Sentinel* (1968). The Spink family established *The Sporting News,* the nation's first all-sports newspaper, on Washington Boulevard in 1886. The feisty *Riverfront Times* appeared in the 1970s. Today stltoday.com and stlbeacon.org offer two different approaches to St. Louis news.

In 1921, Saint Louis University put WEW, the first radio station west of the Mississippi, on the air; it became the city's first FM station in 1955. "The Voice of St. Louis" joined the airwaves on December 24, 1925, adopting the call letters K (the assigned first letter of new radio stations west of the Mississippi), MO (Missouri), and X (Christmas). KMOX pioneered talk radio and call-ins. Currently, its "At Your Service" feature keeps listeners in touch with the city and each other. Starting in the 1950s, a host of DJs on various R&B, rock 'n' roll, and country stations throughout the city have kept the format lively and listeners loyal.

KSD-TV went on the air in 1947; KWK-TV first appeared in 1954, changed to KMOX-TV in 1958, and then, in 1986, became today's KMOV-TV. Early TV was live, ad hoc, and ad lib—a format that fit the medium's pioneers, such as Dave Garroway, Charlotte Peters, and Harry ("Texas Bruce") Gibbs.

Newsies stand ready to fan out across town and sell the *St. Louis Times.* Competition was tough for news sellers in the days when St. Louis had several dailies.

Above: Setting type by hand was laborious work in the years before computers. *Right:* The Post-Dispatch building, home of the city's lone daily today.

Above: A St. Louis Brownie troop watches the first locally produced TV program in 1947.

SPORTS

St. Louisans take their sports seriously. Despite its reputation as "the best baseball town in America," residents participate in many other sports, both as spectators and players. The enjoyment of sports is multigenerational, cross-cultural, and non gender-specific. In other words, anyone can jump up and down in the stands yelling, "Go team!"

The St. Louis Brown Stockings were the first professional baseball team in town, taking the field in 1875. The Brown Stockings morphed into the Cardinals in 1900. In 1902, the St. Louis Browns, a wholly different baseball team, came to the city from Milwaukee. They stayed until 1954, when owner Bill Veeck moved them to Baltimore. Negro League baseball was also active in St. Louis from 1909 to 1943, with the St. Louis Stars the best-known team.

The Chicago football Cardinals (no relation to the baseball team) moved to St. Louis in 1960. During the 1970s, Big Red was also known as "the Cardiac Cardinals" due to exciting last-second wins and frustrating near-wins. After months of acrimony, owner Bill Bidwell moved the franchise to Phoenix in 1988. The Rams came to St. Louis from Los Angeles in 1995, and they won Super Bowl XXXIV in 2000.

Professional basketball was in town from 1955 to 1968 with the St. Louis Hawks. The team won an NBA championship in 1958. The St. Louis Blues was one of six teams added to the National Hockey League in 1967. Its loyal fans are reputed to be the loudest in the League, but so far their loyalty has been unrewarded by a Stanley Cup.

In 2005, to ensure its completion by opening day, construction of the new Busch Stadium proceeded while old Busch was being demolished.

New Busch Stadium is fan-friendly, with tons of amenities and places to spend money.

Jack and Joe Buck are members of the much-loved first family of sportscasting. Jack, associated with every pro sport in the city, was voted into the Baseball Hall of Fame, the National Radio Hall of Fame, and the St. Louis Media Halls of Fame.

The St. Louis Rams host the Carolina Panthers in an exhibition game at the Jones Dome in 2007.

UNION STATION

Theodore Link designed Union Station in 1891 to be extravagant, massive, and strikingly beautiful. It boomed out a welcome, much like the city of St. Louis itself at the turn of the century. Twenty thousand invited guests attended its magnificent opening on September 1, 1894, when the huge chandelier hanging in the Grand Hall sparkled with 350 lamps.

For years, Union Station was a small city with restaurants, sleeping accommodations, changing rooms, and the most elegant waiting rooms one could find. Redcaps and maids hovered. Even the most finicky passengers were awed. Traveler's Aid, an organization begun by St. Louis mayor Bryan Mullanphy to help stranded travelers, also had an office in the station.

In the mid-1890s, more railroad lines (22) converged in St. Louis than in any other city in the United States, including Chicago. On an average day, 1,500 tickets could be sold at Union Station. It had 19 miles of track in the train yards, and the train shed stretched for ten acres.

During World Wars I and II, Union Station was a scene for tearful farewells and joyous reunions. The busiest day in its history was December 22, 1945, when soldiers and new civilians were heading home for the holidays.

After 1950, passenger-train travel slowed to a trickle as air travel took off. Union Station was closed to train travel in 1978 with the departure of the last Amtrak train.

Union Station, 1895

A New Union Station

Union Station was closed from 1978 to 1985 for a $150 million renovation. No longer a train station, it now has fine restaurants, a shopping mall, and a 539-room hotel. The Grand Hall is grand once again and alive with sightseers.

Right: In 1940, the unveiling of "The Meeting of the Waters" statuary group across from Union Station shocked St. Louisans. Designed by Carl Milles to symbolize the confluence of the Mississippi and Missouri rivers, its nude figures were too much for some residents, who called for draping them in opaque material.

SOLDIERS MEMORIAL

The Soldiers Memorial was built in 1936 and dedicated by President Franklin D. Roosevelt to honor those who served in World War I. Many of the Missouri doughboys who went "Over There" in the Great War of 1918 fought in the deadly trenches of Argonne under Lt. Harry Truman. Stone panels between the massive columns of the memorial are carved with the faces of war veterans. On the north and south sides are large stone statues of winged horses and resolute men and women, representing courage, loyalty, vision, and sacrifice.

Across the street from the memorial is a small monument commemorating the 1919 founding of the American Legion. One generation later, in the week after the December 7, 1941, attack on Pearl Harbor, volunteers packed army and navy recruiting stations in the city. Thousands of St. Louisans served their country during World War II in Europe, Africa, and Asia, including WACs, Waves, WAAFs, and American Red Cross "doughnut dollies." The Korean, Vietnam, and Gulf wars did not see the outpouring of patriotism that the world wars did, but the fallen from those wars are honored here as well. Today, the memorial and its museum act as a center for veterans' activities in the city.

In 1940, many people in St. Louis were not aware they were close to another devastating world war. Here soldiers give a KP demonstration.

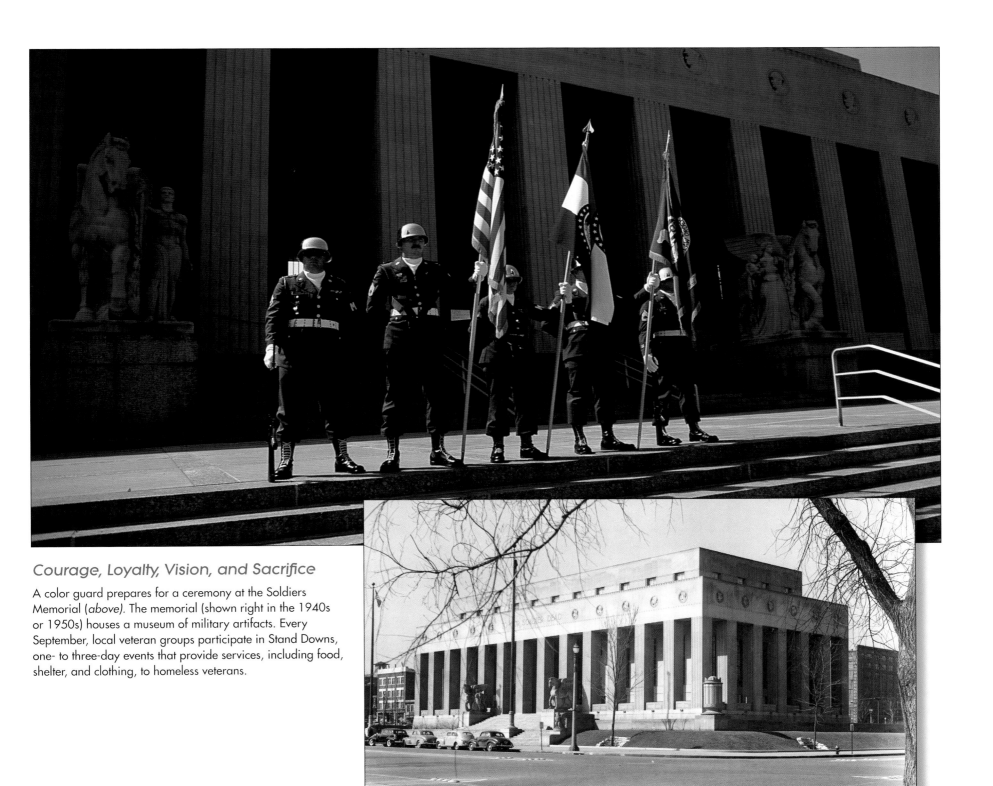

Courage, Loyalty, Vision, and Sacrifice

A color guard prepares for a ceremony at the Soldiers Memorial (*above*). The memorial (shown right in the 1940s or 1950s) houses a museum of military artifacts. Every September, local veteran groups participate in Stand Downs, one- to three-day events that provide services, including food, shelter, and clothing, to homeless veterans.

OLD CATHEDRAL

Shortly after he arrived in 1764, Pierre Laclede dedicated a large block of ground near the riverfront for a Roman Catholic church and planned for a cemetery on the northern half of the block. The first crude log church was completed in 1770, with a slightly more elegant one built in 1776. Appointed as bishop of St. Louis in 1812, one of Father Louis William DuBourg's first priorities was the construction of a cathedral. His successor, Joseph Rosati, carried on his mission and oversaw the completion of the present neoclassical building. It was consecrated in 1834 in a ceremony that drew Catholics from across the United States.

When the new cathedral was built on Lindell Boulevard in 1914, the downtown cathedral, now the "Old Cathedral," officially became the Church of St. Louis of France. For years it was left to deteriorate. In 1959, a major restoration project began, restoring it to its original appearance. In 1961, Pope John XXIII designated the Old Cathedral a basilica, or "public church," stating that it belonged to the world beyond its parish. Its name was changed to the Basilica of Saint Louis, King of France, and the ornamental insignias of a basilica were displayed: the half open umbrella (canopeum) and the bell in the key-shape frame (tintinnabulum).

Above: In 1934, the Old Cathedral was surrounded by buildings. Today, the buildings are gone, and the cathedral stands with the Arch on the Arch grounds. *Right:* On the eve of the cease-fire in Vietnam, January 27, 1973, parishioners pray for peace.

Celebrants at Fair St. Louis surround the Basilica of St. Louis, King of France.

TRANSPORTATION

Erastus Wells provided the city's first horse-drawn public omnibus in 1843. Within a few years there were 90 buses on the streets. Public transportation was popular from the onset, but horse-drawn vehicles were messy and required constant street cleaning. Nonetheless, they persisted into the 20th century; the last horse-drawn fire engine was retired in 1927.

Streetcar tracks were laid throughout the metropolitan area beginning in 1859, and routes were set. Steam-powered cable cars were tried in the 1880s, but they didn't operate well in cold, wet weather. Next came battery-operated streetcars, another short-lived experiment. Electricity provided the best solution. In 1890, the same year that electric streetlights were installed in the city, trolley cars powered by overhead electric wires were put in service. Trolleys lasted for 60 years and are still remembered fondly.

Buggy manufacturer George Dorris was one of several St. Louis residents who saw the potential in horseless carriages in 1898. The popularity of bicycles had already demonstrated that people didn't want to be tied down to streetcar schedules. Half a dozen enthusiastic St. Louis tinkerers built autos in makeshift garages. Dorris Motor Car Company was the most successful, producing 4,000 vehicles between 1906 and 1925.

Eventually, automobiles required paved streets, traffic signals, a larger police force, highways, gasoline stations, and parking garages. Four interstates split the city today, and summertime smog sometimes hangs over the city like a blanket.

Above: In 1910, it was already evident that automobiles would create traffic jams. And where could those cars be parked? *Right:* Horse-drawn vehicles remained on the streets through 1910. The last St. Louis Fire Department horses were retired in 1927.

Right: Passengers in the 1920s filled streetcars and double-decker buses. *Below:* MetroLink light rail plans to expand its lines now that public transportation is back in favor. The system has an average of 68,000 riders each weekday. MetroBus connects with each MetroLink station in Missouri.

LACLEDE'S LANDING

Pierre Laclede probably didn't land in this exact spot in 1764, but he was close enough to lend it his name. Laclede's Landing is the city's only surviving portion of the street pattern laid out in the original survey for the French village. This grid system, similar to that of New Orleans, is made up of rectangular blocks broken up by narrow, cobblestoned streets and alleys.

The Landing has seen many incarnations. The Missouri Fur Company warehouse (also called the Old Rock House), cornerstone of the lucrative fur trade, originated here. It was torn down by the National Park Service in 1939 in order to build the Arch.

In 1840, a mill, a foundry, commercial shops, and places of residence were built on Laclede's Landing. The fire of 1849, which destroyed 15 square blocks of the city, began just south of the Landing, so it was spared. (After the fire, all new construction in St. Louis was iron-fronted, built using brick, stone, or cast-iron skeletons.) In 1880, manufacturers on the Landing included those for stoves, paint, oils, tools, metal stamping, and hides. The Landing was a cluster of dismal warehouses by the mid-20th century and remained so until its rebirth as an entertainment district after the development of the Arch grounds in the 1970s.

Above: Soldiers walk toward the art deco SS *Admiral* in 1941, only a year after her maiden voyage. The huge excursion boat, operated by Joe Streckfus, was longer than a city block and could hold 4,400 passengers on its four decks. It has been moored since 1979 and is now the home of a casino. *Left:* Laclede's Landing was drab and dispirited until the Arch grounds were fully developed in the 1970s.

Laclede's Landing Today

Today most of the remaining buildings on Laclede's Landing have been rehabbed and converted into restaurants, nightclubs, or offices. The Switzer Candy Co. was established on the Landing in 1888, when Mr. Switzer sold licorice from a pushcart. The Switzer building was damaged in the summer storms of 2006 and has since been demolished.

Left: Produce Row in the 1930s was loosely organized, with an informal setting. *Below:* Trucks line up at today's Produce Row, which operates like the big business it is.

PRODUCE ROW

From the rich farmland and orchards of Missouri and Illinois come countless varieties of fruit and vegetables. Commercial buyers gather before dawn at Produce Row in north St. Louis to fill their orders. Much of the harvest goes to chefs working in St. Louis restaurants.

For many years, one of St. Louis's finest restaurants belonged to Tony Faust, son-in-law of Adolphus Busch. More recent favorites were the Catfish and Crystal Restaurant and Miss Hullings' Cafeteria, where the pies were said to hover in the air before landing on your plate.

W.C. HANDY

W.C. (William Christopher) Handy was born in 1873 in Alabama. He studied music throughout school and in college, becoming the bandleader of the touring show, Mahara's Minstrels, in 1890. After forming his own band in 1905, he toured the southern states for many years, moving to New York City in 1917 to start a music publishing company and a recording company. Handy took part in the black cultural movement, the Harlem Renaissance, and came to be known as the "father of the blues" for bringing blues songs such as his "St. Louis Blues" and "Memphis Blues" to the public's attention. He died in March 1958.

MUSIC

"I hate to see that evenin' sun go down," the haunting wail that opens "St. Louis Blues" is one of the most familiar melodies in blues music. W. C. Handy didn't spend much time in St. Louis because he couldn't find work—a sure enough reason for the blues—but the city inspired him to write the classic. "Frankie and Johnnie," another bluesy narrative, was born in St. Louis at the Rosebud Café, where Tom Turpin introduced his patrons to Scott Joplin's rags. Dixieland, brassy and bold, got toes tapping on showboats and enlivened the march lines in parades along the levee. After World War II, Russ David's romantic slow-dancing band softened the atmosphere for a while—until duck-walking, guitar-tossing Chuck Berry and the electronic thumping of Ike and Tina Turner gave the city rock 'n' roll.

After completion in 1934, Kiel Opera House was the city's major performing arts center for 30 years. It is now vacant, but rumors continue to circulate about its rebirth.

EADS BRIDGE

As a young boy, instead of attending school, James Eads sold apples on the streets of St. Louis in order to help his family. Always an entrepreneur, Eads developed a salvage business when he was a young man, going underwater to bring up usable parts of wrecked riverboats. To do so, he constructed a diving bell that allowed him to walk along the shifting river bottom. In the process, he learned hydraulics and became an expert on the dangers of the river. When the Civil War began, the U.S. Army sought out Eads for advice on securing the Mississippi for the Union. He suggested armor-plated gunboats. These "ironclads" were built in record time, many at the Carondelet shipyards, and they succeeded in keeping the Confederacy from militarizing the lower Mississippi.

After the Civil War, Eads turned his attention to designing a railroad bridge across the river at St. Louis. An engineering marvel, Eads Bridge was almost ten years in the making, from conception to completion. Its massive three-span, two-level design was innovative in every respect. Eads insisted that the foundations for the bridge rest on bedrock to ensure stability in the unpredictable river current, requiring workers to go 136 feet below water on the east pier. Eads invented a sand pump and improved his airlock designs and diving bell. Nonetheless, 14 men died of the bends while working underwater.

The Eads Bridge opened to much fanfare on July 4, 1874, and at last St. Louis entered the railroad age.

The engineering involved in constructing the Eads Bridge is as impressive as that of the aqueducts of Rome.

Eads Bridge Innovation

When shipping by river was as important as by rail or truck, the levee below Eads Bridge was rarely empty *(right)*. Today, the refurbished Eads Bridge has a pedestrian walkway on the upper level; the light rail MetroLink uses the lower level *(below)*.

South City: St. Louis Melting Pot

For the most part, the people who settled south of St. Louis were Europeans: brave souls who dared to leave all that was familiar for a dream. They brought with them recipes, music, stories, and a willingness to work hard—but little else. Most were Catholic, but a substantial number were Protestant, Jewish, or Freethinker. The men usually came first. Not well-educated or highly skilled, they took any job they could find and lived in primitive boarding houses, often without running water or heat. Faithfully, they sent their money home so that eventually their families could follow.

A 1953 South City neighborhood, home to the legendary "scrubby Dutch."

Few of these new immigrants could speak English well, if at all. The culture shock was just that—a shock—and they needed each other to survive in this strange country. They formed neighborhoods, each with its own distinct culture. Usually the centerpiece was a church, or occasionally a synagogue. Religious institutions, social clubs, and educational societies held them together and allowed them to Americanize. They were not raised with democracy, but they took to it immediately.

The children of these immigrants were 100 percent American—maybe 110 percent—a source of both pride and anguish. To the second generation, the future was more important than tradition (the past). They were ambitious, found work at an early age, aimed for college or technical school, and had dreams outside the neighborhood. Today, much of south St. Louis has become homogenized, but some of the old threads can still be seen.

DIVERSE SETTLERS

The first area to be settled south of the city was Soulard, south of present-day Chouteau and east of Jefferson Avenue to the river. In the late 18th century, wealthy French families built houses

A brewhouse worker checks the product in 1938—brewing beer has been a major South City occupation for almost 200 years.

along present-day Broadway, then the road to the established village of Carondelet. Nearby was a ferry landing at the end of Arsenal Street, which connected them with Cahokia, also a French town.

Beginning in the 1830s, Germans began arriving in the city and found modest and affordable housing just west of Broadway. These small brick and frame homes were constructed with narrow gangways between them and, in typical European style, built adjacent to sidewalks without front yards.

Breweries were being built in the area, taking advantage of the many caves that could keep the beer cool year-round. Jobs were to be had, not only as brewers, but also as coopers, draymen, and tavern owners. Over the next 50 years, free blacks, Bohemians (Czechs), Serbs, Syrians, Hungarians, Poles, and Slavs joined Germans and the French in Soulard, making it one of the most polyglot neighborhoods in the nation.

Northwest of Soulard was Lafayette Square—originally part of a Spanish land grant. In the mid-19th century, wealthy native St. Louisans escaped the noise and smells of the city by moving north, west, or south. In South City, they built large Victorian homes fronting Lafayette Park. Just west of Lafayette Square, sinkholes and caves in the area hampered the development of Benton Park. By the 1890s, most had been filled in; small, single-family dwellings and large homes were built for the middle class.

Both Lafayette Park and Soulard caught the brunt of the deadly tornado of 1896, when 138 people were killed and thousands injured. The tornado destroyed a mile-wide area of buildings, uprooting hundreds of trees and causing $2.9 billion worth of damage in today's dollars. The area was rebuilt, but Lafayette Park never again had the prestige it once enjoyed.

A PIECE OF ITALY

The neighborhood that has kept its distinctive character for more than one hundred years is the Hill, west of Kingshighway and south of Arsenal. Clay deposits were discovered in the area in the late 1830s. When the Pacific Railroad was completed to Cheltenham in 1852, St. Louis Smelting and Refining Company was built, attracting German and Irish immigrants. During the 1890s, Italian men came by the hundreds to find work there.

At first they lived in a raggedy area of Fairmont, in frame houses without city services. As they became more prosperous, their families arrived, and neighborhoods of neat brick homes with front yards and backyards were built. Corner groceries, butchers, bakeries, barbershops, tailors, and cobblers followed. St. Ambrose Roman Catholic Church was built in 1903. Today, three quarters of the neighborhood still boasts of its Italian heritage. The area is noted for its excellent restaurants.

The gracious Lafayette neighborhood had one of the city's first public parks, shown here between 1870 and 1900.

On the northern edge of the Hill, several public institutions were built: the City Sanitarium (later the State Lunatic Asylum), County Poor Farm (which eventually became the Truman Restorative Center), Female Hospital (originally the Social Evil Hospital for the treatment of venereal diseases), the Missouri State School for Retarded Children, and the State Hospital for the Insane. Today, the St. Louis Psychiatric Rehabilitation Center on Arsenal is the only remaining institution of the original cluster.

A NEIGHBORHOOD FOR ALL

The Marquette-Cherokee neighborhood southeast of the Hill was laid out in 1836. Even before builders arrived, the streets running north and south were named for the states of the Union and those running east-west were named for various Native American Nations. It was an area of farms, orchards, and grape arbors until the 1880s, when residential and commercial development began.

First came modest brick homes for working-class families. Shops, theaters, and small businesses congregated along Virginia Avenue and Cherokee. Day or night, the streets were alive, as they are today: Antique shops and vintage clothing stores tempt customers with nostalgia, quality used furniture, and junk. A growing Hispanic population has created "Little Mexico" on the eastern end of Cherokee, home of the largest Cinco de Mayo celebration in St. Louis.

Soulard and live music go together like red beans and rice.

RALSTON-PURINA

William Danforth was a sickly farm boy in southeast Missouri when a schoolteacher challenged him to become "the healthiest boy in the class." He took the dare—living 85 healthy years—and subsequently built his life on the principles he cherished: Aspire nobly, adventure daringly, and serve humbly.

The Panic of 1893 hit shortly after Danforth graduated from Washington University, and he realized that no matter how the economy fluctuated, animals must eat. In 1894, he began mixing formula feed for farm animals. He chose the name Purina from his slogan, "Purity is Paramount," and the red and white checkerboard logo for its distinctiveness. When Purina expanded to include cereal for people, it took the Ralston name from a doctor who recommended eating cooked, cracked-wheat cereal for good health. Cowboy star Tom Mix became the spokesman for Ralston cereal, and generations of children learned the secret Straight Shooters handshake and password after mailing box tops to Checkerboard Square in St. Louis.

After 1950, Ralston-Purina entered the massive pet market, creating "chows" for virtually every variety. In the 1980s, it bought several food-related and non food-related companies, including Continental Baking Company and Eveready Batteries. In the 1990s, it entered the global marketplace with enthusiasm, but its high profile attracted the giant Nestlé Corporation, which bought it in 2001.

The Purina Checkerboard

The Ralson-Purina headquarters shows off its company's unique checkerboard pattern in 1947 *(above)*. Today, the Purina building is more modern, with less red and white, but the headquarters is still located in the area of St. Louis known as Checkerboard Square *(right)*. Purina Farms, located outside downtown St. Louis, has a tourist center, competition areas, and provides activities and exhibits that help strengthen the bond between pet owners and their furry friends. Purina also sponsors various events all over the country, such as dog shows and pet comedy challenges.

On January 10, 1962, at 3:23 P.M., a freak explosion ripped apart the giant mill of Ralston-Purina, sending 1,000 employees out into the bitter cold. Three people died and 35 were hospitalized in the five-alarm fire. Water turned to ice almost as soon as it left the fire hoses.

SOULARD MARKET

In the 1780s, Gabriel Cerre developed his land grant as a fruit orchard south of St. Louis. He deeded it to his daughter, Julia, and her husband, Antoine Soulard. They, in turn, carved up the property for their children. In 1838, Julia gave the city a site for a perpetual farmer's market, which has always been called Soulard Market. A building for the market was first erected in 1843. The monster tornado of 1896 smashed the two-story section. It was repaired, but a new structure wasn't built until 1929. A hospital for abandoned children in Florence is said to be the model for its Italian Renaissance style. The market today has two flanking market stall structures with a two-story central building. Its second floor contains an auditorium and a stage.

Visitors to the market find not only tomatoes, onions, and celery, but a variety of locally grown, processed, caught, or handcrafted items, such as fish, jewelry, bakery goods, boiled peanuts, soap, flowers, pasta, mushrooms, and unusual meats.

The Soulard neighborhood has transformed itself several times, from Frenchtown to Germantown to possibly the most multi-ethnic enclave in the city. Its creative use of architecture is legendary. Churches have become gyms, restaurants, and theaters; a former police station became an art museum; a fire station became an office; factories and warehouses were turned into lofts. What has not changed is the number of taverns per block.

In 1952, the path of the new Interregional Highway was routed specifically to avoid Soulard Market; here, in 1955, it's business as usual.

If You Can't Find It at Soulard Market . . .

…it's probably not edible. The market has changed very little over the years, adding exotic fruits and veggies as customers call for them. The last public market in the city of St. Louis, it is open year-round. The market is next to a park and is used for different neighborhood events. The year "1779" on the sign is somewhat of a mystery. It could refer to a previous market that may or may not have existed in the surrounding area in 1779, when St. Louis was just a village.

BREWERIES

The story of brewing in St. Louis began in 1810 with a beer advertisement: $5 cash or $6 in produce per barrel from Jacques St. Vrain's Bellefontaine Brewery. Small breweries came and went until Johann (Adam) Lemp discovered a way to make lager—the light, clear beer that Americans preferred (and still do) to the heavy, dark European brews. A combination of plentiful water supply, underground caves where ice from the frozen Mississippi kept beer cold year-round ("lagering" it), and lots of thirsty German residents made St. Louis a brewing paradise by the mid-19th century.

Eberhard Anheuser's Bavarian Brewery was one of about 50 breweries in the city when his son-in-law, Adolphus Busch, joined it in 1870. Busch was not a brewer and actually preferred wine to beer, but he was a genius at marketing. Adam Lemp's son, William, and Busch chased each other to get the lion's share of the American market. They built bottling facilities and, by using new refrigerated cars, devised shipping schedules that kept beer fresh. They developed advertising campaigns, slogans, and logos. Busch introduced Budweiser and Michelob; Lemp, Falstaff. Both men expanded their breweries, built elegant mansions, and lived extravagantly. Both left their empires to sons who struggled during Prohibition. Both sons, William Lemp, Jr., and August A. Busch, committed suicide.

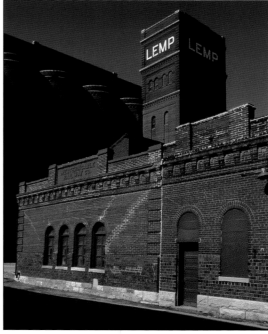

Above: The Anheuser-Busch brewery was back to work in 1934, the year after Prohibition was repealed. *Right:* The two-dozen buildings and 15 acres of the Lemp Brewery, vacant for years, are slated to be rehabbed for commercial use. Adam Lemp established his brewery in 1838 and claimed to have created the first lager in town.

Anheuser-Busch Goes Belgian

After several weeks of high drama in the summer of 2008, the Anheuser-Busch board of directors voted to accept a buy-out from the Belgian giant InBev. Budweiser trucks are found in virtually every city in the world *(above)*, delivering dozens of A-B brands, including Michelob ULTRA Pomegranate Raspberry and Tuscan Orange Grapefruit. Inside, brass glows in the immaculate Anheuser-Busch brewhouse *(right)*.

PROHIBITION

Prohibition was disastrous for St. Louis and an insult to the city's Italians, Irish, and Germans. The amendment, which made the manufacture, sale, and/or transportation of alcohol a federal crime, was defeated in the city, but voters in rural Missouri overrode the city's vote and joined the majority of Americans who voted "dry." On January 16, 1920, a major St. Louis industry was shut down and thousands of people put out of work. There was no question of obeying the law; the only question was how to get around it. The city's gangs, especially Egan's Rats and Sicilian Green Ones, began a battle for supremacy in the bootleg market. Street shoot-outs were common; between 1920 and 1930, 46 police officers died in the line of duty, more than in any other decade in the history of the St. Louis Police Department.

When Prohibition was repealed in March 1933, jubilant St. Louisans gathered at the Anheuser-Busch brewery to celebrate. Adolphus Busch III sent a case of Budweiser to President Roosevelt. The Lemp Brewery had not been able to withstand Prohibition; Joseph Griesedieck bought the Falstaff name for $25,000. His brothers produced Griesedieck Brothers beer ("Slippery Richard"), one of the most popular local beers until the company was sold in 1955. Today, Griesedieck Brothers is back as a microbrewery, along with the Schlafly label of the fast-growing St. Louis Brewery.

This bootlegger was caught in the act during Prohibition. Raids by federal agents couldn't keep up with the vast amounts of bootlegging that occurred.

A.B.C. and Excelsior Breweries were two of the dozens of breweries in the city in the 19th century, when it was customary to give brewery employees a tin pail of beer to help the workday along.

Mom-and-pop stores, such as this one shown here in 1943, were the forerunners of today's convenience mini-marts.

CHEROKEE STREET

A busy six-block commercial district sprang up when streetcar lines reached Cherokee Street in the 1890s. Shoppers crowded into the many stores for dry goods, shoes, furniture, and groceries. If none of those products tickled their fancy, there were always dime stores, confectionaries, and saloons. Service providers such as butchers, cleaners, tailors, jewelers, photographers, barbers, druggists, and dentists could also be found. Proprietors frequently lived above their stores, giving the street a homey feel. Frank Bick began the *South Side Journal* on Cherokee Street. Fred Wehrenberg opened a motion picture theater there in 1906 and later built an outdoor movie theater called an airdome. A skating rink, a beer garden, and the Casa Loma Ballroom also drew St. Louisans searching for entertainment. The surrounding neighborhood was working class—many residents were employed at the nearby Lemp Brewery—and was made up of four-family flats and small, one-story "railroad houses."

In the 1950s, buses replaced the Cherokee streetcar lines. At the same time, shoppers left city neighborhoods for the more modern shopping centers and supermarkets farther west. By the 1970s, the Cherokee area was almost deserted. J.C. Penney, Woolworth's, and Kresge's had moved out. What saved the street was America's love for the past: Antique stores and retro-clothing shops took over. The area gained a reputation for being "quaint," and bargain hunters from throughout the Midwest streamed in. The Antique Row Association fought for clean sidewalks and buildings. Unique restaurants and pubs arrived. Today, the west section of Cherokee Street is home to "Little Mexico." Piñatas hang in shop windows and the smell of empanadas wafts through the air.

Left: Empire Sandwich shop, once a Cherokee Street landmark, was demolished in the spring of 2006. *Below:* Today, antique stores along Cherokee Street draw bargain hunters from throughout the Midwest.

CARONDELET

In 1767, the Frenchman Clement DeLore de Treget established his family estate on a plateau between Sainte Genevieve and St. Louis. Other French families joined him, and they formed a village. In 1794, they named it in honor of Baron Francois Louis Hector de Carondelet, the governor of Louisiana.

From the 1840s to the 1980s, Carondelet had a strong industrial base. First came a manufacturer of lead shot— Vulcan Iron Works was built in 1858. More iron works were established after the Iron Mountain Railway brought ore directly from the St. Francois Mountains. Docks were built with facilities for shipbuilding and ship repair. During the Civil War, James B. Eads oversaw the building of ironclads and gunboats at Eads Union Marine Works. Eventually, the company became St. Louis Ship-Federal Barge, one of the nation's largest producers of barges and river towboats and the operator of Federal Barge Lines, a quasi-government operation that closed around 2001. Today, the Carondelet riverfront is almost deserted.

Top: All of these buildings were present in late 19th century Carondelet. One of the first buildings in the town belonged to the Sisters of St. Joseph of Carondelet, who founded St. Joseph's Academy and Fontbonne College (now University). *Right:* The view from Bellerive Park on the bluffs of South Broadway encompasses much of the Mississippi River valley. The park was named for St. Ange de Bellerive, the first French commandant at St. Louis.

BEVO MILL

On opening day in 1917, Bevo Mill awaits customers. The U.S. flags on the tables during that war year emphasized that even though they were serving German food, their hearts were American.

August A. Busch decided to build Bevo Mill for several reasons. He wanted to establish a family restaurant on busy Gravois Boulevard where alcohol and meals could be served to working-class adults and where children were welcome—a place unlike either a neighborhood tavern or a high-class, expensive restaurant. He also wanted a refreshment stop that was halfway between his brewery and his home at Grant's Farm. And he loved windmills. The restaurant was opened in 1917, and after a brief closure, is back in operation today.

Bevo Mill was named for Bevo, the beer-flavored, nonalcoholic drink that Busch brewers concocted. Its name was probably chosen because it sounded like "pivo," the Slavic word for beer. Interestingly enough, the Bevo Mill neighborhood is now the premier Slavic-speaking (Bosnian) neighborhood in the city.

Bevo Mill as it appeared in 1955 and as it is today.

THE HILL

While early immigrants from southern Italy mostly settled downtown, northern Italians headed for *La Montagna*. But 50 years before the Italian settlement of the Hill, a group of French socialists tried to create a utopia there. Etienne Cabet, with his group of idealist Icarians, purchased a 28-acre site on Wilson Avenue in 1853. They built a commune made up of small cabins where they planned to enjoy drama, music, and literature. But they were not prepared for isolation, difficult St. Louis weather, or the reality of meeting financial obligations. In 1864, after much dissension, the group broke up, and the site was abandoned.

Italians, determined to succeed in America, found the site more congenial. Despite their geographic rivalries (Milanese versus Lombardi, for instance), they wanted to take care of their own. In 1866, Genoans founded *La Societa Unione e Fratellanza Italiana* to help fellow immigrants adjust to their new home. When St. Ambrose Church was established in 1903, it became the center of neighborhood life, where residents celebrated christenings, first communions, weddings, and all the other milestones, with parties spilling over into homes and restaurants.

Sports have also held the community together. There are two bocce gardens. Baseball greats Yogi Berra and Joe Garagiola lived across the street from each other and both worked as waiters at Ruggeri's Restaurant. The book and docudrama *The Game of Their Lives* (re-titled *The Miracle Match*) tells the story of the U.S. soccer team that defeated England in 1950; most of the team members came from the Hill.

In 1917, houses in the Hill were mostly shotgun shanties—thin, rectangular houses where one room leads into another without a hallway. Railroad houses could also be found: Built like a railroad car, the home was set up as a hallway with small rooms along the sides.

St. Ambrose: The Community Center

Hopeful Italian immigrants are movingly commemorated in this statue located at St. Ambrose Church *(above)*. The church is a fixture of the Italian-American community; in 1955, St. Ambrose's parish was redefined from a national to a territorial one—the parish now encompasses the Hill. Today, Columbus Day is celebrated on the Hill with a parade that passes by St. Ambrose *(right)*. Red, white, and green flags, awnings, and fire hydrants speak to the neighborhood's pride in its Italian heritage.

SAUERBRATEN AND PAD THAI

German influence on St. Louis can hardly be overstated. Many German immigrants left their homeland for the American Midwest after the failed revolution of 1848 and became strong advocates for democracy and freedom of expression. They established newspapers—the *Westliche Post* was the most prominent—and philosophical journals. The *Vereine,* or social societies, were known for their *Gemütlichkeit* (friendliness and conviviality), and St. Louisans enjoyed visiting the many German beer gardens. In 1860, about 60 percent of St. Louis residents were of German heritage. They did not live in enclaves as other ethnic groups did, but they spread throughout the area, from Hermann to Belleville. After the Civil War, German Jews dominated the garment business; German Lutherans established social service agencies and joined craft unions; German Catholics founded numerous schools. Strong anti-German sentiment at the beginning of World War I made many German Americans downplay their heritage and ended the use of German in schools and churches.

Today's South City immigrants are from Asia, the Middle East, Africa, and Bosnia. On South Grand, between Arsenal and Utah streets, a strip of shops and restaurants has grown to cater to this international clientele. The majority represent southeast Asia—Vietnam, Laos, Cambodia, and Thailand.

Some Chinese came to St. Louis in the late 19th century. A Chinatown called Hop Alley developed downtown, with shops, restaurants, and residences. The entire area was demolished for the first Busch Stadium in 1964. A modest number of Japanese made their home in St. Louis in the years before 1940. After the Japanese attack on Pearl Harbor in 1941, and the subsequent declaration of war, all Japanese were rounded up and interned in one of the nation's many camps. Fortunately, most returned to the city of St. Louis, and many more have joined them. A large Hindu temple in West County serves part of the growing Indian population.

Wreath of Songs

In 1953, The Liederkranz, the popular German cultural and singing society, met in this building at 13th and Chouteau. Many German social clubs and *turnvereins* (gymnastic societies) were scattered throughout the city. *Liederkranz* means "wreath of songs," underscoring the German love of music and dance.

Left: A German band entertains in 1937, perhaps at a beer garden during Maifest or Oktoberfest. *Below:* Multiethnic restaurants, gift shops, and grocery stores line South Grand Boulevard, between Arsenal and Utah streets.

SHAW'S GARDEN

Henry Shaw loved trees . . . and tulips, baby's breath, lilies, cacti, and turnips. Whether exotic or homegrown, all plants fascinated Shaw. Only 19 years old when he arrived in St. Louis from England in 1819, Shaw set up a hardware store downtown, selling high quality cutlery and other metal products. He made a fortune and retired when he was 40. From that point, he was able to engage in his real life's work—beautifying his corner of the earth. Today's Tower Grove Park was a prairie when he chose it for his country estate. By the time he died in 1889, the 285-acre park had thousands of trees and was laid out as an English walking garden with curving paths winding through lush flower beds.

The remainder of Shaw's estate, almost 8,000 acres, along with his extensive library and herbarium, was donated to the city after his death, becoming the Missouri Botanical Garden. In 1959, a large geodesic dome called the "Climatron," designed by Buckminster Fuller, was built to house tropical vegetation. Since 1971, under the leadership of Peter Raven, the garden has grown globally. *Time* magazine named Raven "A Hero for the Planet" because of his advocacy for sustainable growth and conservation of resources. Today, the garden sponsors hundreds of scientists throughout the world, and its TROPICOS database provides instant access to research on millions of plants.

Above: Shown here in 1935, the Palm House conservatory was built for the park's tropical plants, which enhanced the lawns in the summer and were displayed in the conservatory during the winter. *Right:* Corky the Clown (Clif St. James) entertains children at the garden in the early 1970s.

Missouri Botanical Garden

The Climatron geodesic dome provides a tropical environment year-round for its approximately 1,200 species of plants. Blown glass Walla Wallas by artist Dale Chihuly and bronze scupltures by Carl Milles enhance the reflecting pool.

The Kaeser Maze at the garden is a favorite with children.

COMPTON HILL RESERVOIR PARK

In the 1890s, St. Louis was growing so fast the water system couldn't keep up with it. A standpipe was erected on Compton Hill to equalize the water pressure coming from the north side, but the pipe was deemed too ugly for the nearby upper-class neighborhood. In 1898, a 180-foot, French Romanesque tower was constructed to camouflage the pipe. Its base was decorated with a griffin and swirling vines; a single, asymmetrical turret gave it distinction. Around its diameter was a spiral iron staircase, made up of 198 steps, that led up to an observation platform where thousands of visitors admired a view of the city. Set in the middle of Reservoir Park, the tower instantly became a South City landmark, visible for miles.

By 1929, the city's water system was modernized and the standpipe was no longer needed. The Compton Hill Water Tower was closed to visitors, except for an occasional tour. In 1972, local historians were successful in getting it listed on the National Register of Historic Places. Asbestos was discovered inside the tower in 1984; it was abandoned and left to deteriorate for years. In the mid-1990s, preservationists organized to save it from demolition. A $19 million renovation was completed in 1999 and celebrated with a giant block party. Today, the Water Tower and Park Preservation Society is planning to restore the park—severely diminished by I-44—and recreate the historic landscape with its Victorian ponds and fountains.

The Compton Hill Water Tower stands sentinel over a lily pond in the original park in 1909.

Above: Gates to the distinctive Compton Heights neighborhood and historic district, where Longfellow, Hawthorne, and Milton avenues invite a leisurely discussion of metaphor and symbolism in literature. *Left:* The water tower has been repaired and renovated and is prepared to remain standing for another hundred years.

LAFAYETTE SQUARE

When it came time to name the city's first park in 1836, the memory of the visit of Marquis de Lafayette of France 12 years earlier must have come to the fore. He was in St. Louis for only one day, but it was a thrilling one. Scores of residents were waiting at the dock to greet the hero when his steamboat arrived on April 28, 1824. Nine carriages and a company of light horsemen took his party to the mansion of Pierre Chouteau for a public reception. After the reception, Lafayette visited William Clark's Indian Museum and met with a group of Osage. That evening, everyone who could secure an invitation attended a magnificent ball for the Marquis at the Mansion House Hotel. At midnight, like Cinderella, Lafayette left for his steamboat.

Perhaps the planners of the Lafayette Square neighborhood intended to echo that sense of graciousness and elegance, although its development had to wait until after the Civil War. Broad streets surround the 30-acre park, making it feel protected from the city's traffic. In 1868, Jesse Benton Fremont unveiled the statue of her father, Senator Thomas Hart Benton, in Lafayette Park. The statue portrays Benton in a Roman toga and was sculpted by Harriet Hosmer, who was allowed to study anatomy at St. Louis Medical School—albeit segregated from the male students.

Lafayette Square was devastated by the tornado of May 27, 1896. Exploding gas lights started fires that were extinguished by the driving rain—one of the few blessings of the storm. City Hospital was torn apart by the wind, making the treatment of victims difficult. In all, the tornado caused millions of dollars of structural damage, as well as the deaths of 138 people.

Lafayette Square Architecture

Second Empire houses such as these were built between 1855 and 1885. Their distinguishing characteristics include a mansard roof with dormer windows, wrought iron ornamentation, and tall first-floor windows. Lafayette Square is also home to "painted ladies," Victorian-style houses painted in discreet (never flashy) colors.

SOUTH CITY CUISINE

Ted Drewes Frozen Custard is more than a St. Louis tradition; it's an addiction. Drewes opened his first stand on South Grand in 1931 and another one on Chippewa ten years later. Since then, thousands of sugar fans have waited patiently in line on steamy summer evenings for their chance to decide among the 28 flavors (butterscotch? pistachio? mocha? a little of each?). Concretes (frozen custard, "hard as concrete") are often the first choice, with sundaes a close second.

The South City has a rich history of food beyond Steak 'n' Shake, White Castle, and Hodak's fried chicken. The connoisseur can sample brain sandwiches—found everywhere in St. Louis after the appearance of city stockyards in the 1880s. Once a source of fascination for former *Post-Dispatch* columnist Elaine Viets, who focused on local issues and human-interest stories, the demand has dwindled today, but they can still be found on a few menus. Mama Campisi's in the Hill is credited with inventing toasted ravioli—by accidentally dropping the ravioli into hot oil instead of hot water, a chef ended up creating hors d'oeuvres par excellence. Soft and chewy hand-twisted pretzels have been around at Gus' Pretzels since the 1920s, along with his signature bratwurst, salsiccia, and hot dog pretzel sandwiches (don't hold the mustard). Imo's Pizza was founded in 1964 and became an instant "square" tradition. In the 1960s, teenaged heaven was a chuck-with-slaw, dripping with barbeque sauce, from Chuck-a-Burger, followed by a movie at Ronnie's Drive-in with a box of popcorn and a Vess soda.

Cakes from Federhofer's Bakery have made hundreds of weddings, birthdays, and graduations a little sweeter.

Ted Drewes is always crowded, but people don't seem to mind waiting for their turn at the window.

Uncle Bill's is a favorite South City meeting place 24 hours a day—especially in the wee hours.

Setting the Stage for the Grand White Way

In the spring of 1861, after news of the firing on Fort Sumter reached residents, tension filled the city. No one could escape the fact of war, not even the wealthy residents of Lucas Place. The area that would become Midtown, the city's second downtown, was a place of unrest. The large German population was outspoken in their opposition to slavery. Many Yankee Protestants also detested the "peculiar institution." The Irish sided with the Confederacy. There was also a large contingent of St. Louisans who had moved north from the Carolinas and Virginia. Some brought slaves with them and saw no reason to give up their property. Freeborn blacks lived in the area, as well as freed slaves. Many blacks had dared to attend John Berry Meacham's illegal floating school on a Mississippi riverboat, making some white residents nervous about the possibility of insurrection.

Missouri couldn't make up its mind: stick with the Union or join the Confederacy. The governor, Clairborne Jackson, was pro-Confederacy, while St. Louis Congressman Frank Blair was pro-Union. On May 10, 1861, less than a month after the onset of the Civil War, 900 members of the Southern Guard met at Grand and Lindell boulevards, a site they named Camp Jackson. Union forces were ready. Led by Captain Nathaniel Lyon, about 6,000 men marched toward the rebels. The city's population gathered to watch the confrontation. U.S. soldiers rounded up members of the Southern Guard, who barely protested, while Confederate sympathizers threw rocks at the soldiers, beginning a bloody riot. Twenty-eight people died and many more were wounded. It took many years for St. Louis to recover from the bitterness of that period.

MAKING MIDTOWN

Saint Louis University bought the site of Camp Jackson in 1867 and built its first building, DuBourg Hall, there in 1888. Bishop Louis William DuBourg had founded St. Louis Academy downtown in 1818. The school was transferred to the Jesuits in 1829, who recorded Charles Chouteau, a descendant of the founding family of St. Louis, as one of its first students. Today, the SLU campus stretches from one edge of Midtown to the other.

VOLUNTEERS ATTACKED IN ST. LOUIS.

This 1861 wood engraving depicts the attack on Union Army volunteers at Camp Jackson.

TRIAL AND ERROR

On the eastern edge of Midtown in the early 20th century was Mill Creek Valley. Southern blacks who came to St. Louis after 1920 looking for work—especially those who joined the workforce during World War II—found they were allowed to live in very few places in the city. Mill Creek Valley was one area sanctioned for them. There, inhabitants built small wooden houses and created a close-knit and self-contained neighborhood with grocers, hairdressers and barber shops, variety stores, and restaurants. In the mid-1950s, Mill Creek Valley was declared an urban blight and leveled, its population dispersed.

Perhaps to compensate, Laclede Town was built near the site of the old neighborhood. This planned, integrated community received national attention as an answer to urban tensions. During the 1960s and 1970s, arts groups flourished in Laclede Town, and

disputes were handled by committee rather than confrontation. But by the mid-1980s, vandalism and illegal drugs trade had disintegrated the dream, and Laclede Town was closed. Today, the former A.G. Edwards/Wachovia Securities and Saint Louis University occupy part of the site.

Lindell Boulevard west of the university became home to several social and benevolent organizations: the Elks, Scottish Rite Masons, Shriners, Optimists, and Red Cross among them. The Melbourne, Coronado, and Beers hotels were in the area, but they didn't compete well with downtown hotels.

GRAND ENTERTAINMENT

The intersections of Grand and Lindell and of Grand and Olive, easily reached by streetcar from all directions, seemed perfect for commercial development in the late 19th century. Dubbed "Midtown," it soon became the entertainment

The Moolah Temple on Lindell was built in 1912 for the Shriners. Totally restored today, its large-screen movie theater seats 400 patrons in leather sofas and loveseats. It also houses a bowling alley, bar, and lounge.

Above left: Your Father's Mustache was a popular place for live music in Gaslight Square in 1966. *Above right:* The Grand Forest Apartments were built in Mill Creek Valley in 1964 after the land clearance of the mid-1950s.

district. In the early 20th century, the area was alive with vaudeville shows, burlesque, and moving-picture houses. Multimillion dollar theaters tried to outdo each other in lavishness and luxury. Some were even air-conditioned. *The Jazz Singer* ("Jolson talks!") opened at the Grand Central in 1927, and the world premier of *Meet Me in St. Louis* was held at Loew's State in 1944. During World War II, the lights of the "Grand White Way" never dimmed.

After the war, the area began to decline as suburbia flourished. Neighborhood theaters supplanted the great movie houses. In the late 1950s and early 1960s, many theaters closed and a seedy aura settled over this section of the once-grand Grand Bou-

levard. The beacon atop the majestic Continental Building was turned off as it went into foreclosure.

But miracles happen. In 1965, the Saint Louis Symphony Orchestra bought the run-down RKO St. Louis Theater and renovated it. Encouraged by the SLSO's success in bringing people to Midtown, Fox Associates bought the Fox Theatre in 1981, restored it, and called it "The Fabulous Fox." Since then, art museums, restaurants, and more theaters have opened; the restored Continental Building's penthouse has tenants; and Saint Louis University landscaped its campus to become more inviting. Laughter, applause, and the sound of an orchestra tuning up are heard on North Grand once again.

MILL CREEK VALLEY

Toward the end of the 19th century, African Americans—newly freed from slavery—moved into Mill Creek Valley, which stretched from Tucker to Grand along Market Street. Chestnut Valley, the section of Mill Creek Valley around present-day Union Station, was home to honky-tonks and sporting houses. Ragtime and the blues grew up there; it's where Frankie and Johnny were lovers. When the World's Fair was being planned in 1903, City Beautiful organizers shut down Chestnut Valley and turned out its red lights.

In the late 1950s, St. Louis officials declared that the Mill Creek Valley area west of Jefferson was a blight on the city. By then, it was home to some 20,000 African Americans, and they protested. Nonetheless, the huge area, with its houses, apartment buildings, schools, shops, churches, and taverns was cleared without compensation to the population. Because of de facto segregated housing, blacks were squeezed into the north side, which was emptying out as veterans used VA loans to move to the suburbs.

Sidney Maestre, of Mercantile Trust Company, and Mayor Raymond Tucker look over Mill Creek Valley as "urban renewal" began in 1956. The Land Clearance for Redevelopment Authority (LCRA) hoped to develop the area, but for years the area was called Hiroshima Flats.

Wachovia Securities employed thousands of workers and trained financial advisors. Wachovia's merger with Wells Fargo may bring changes to the financial campus.

THE FINANCIAL CAMPUS

A.G. (Albert Gallatin) Edwards and his son, Benjamin Franklin Edwards, founded a downtown brokerage firm in 1887, after the elder Edwards retired from the post of assistant secretary of the U.S. Treasury. At first the firm worked primarily with Wall Street and St. Louis banks while slowly reaching out to a national market and individual investors. It survived the stock market crash of 1929 through its conservative policies; during the 1930s it adopted the slogan, "Buy a Share in America." As investment expanded worldwide and technology changed financial management, A.G. Edwards kept pace, sometimes leading the pack. The last Edwards retired as president in 2007. Almost immediately thereafter, Wachovia Securities acquired the firm. In 2008, Wachovia itself merged with Wells Fargo.

Laclede Town in the 1960s was an urban utopia—a diverse group of residents lived together and prospered.

LACLEDE TOWN

Several years after the demolition of Mill Creek Valley, a new development began to emerge on the site. Progressive labor leader Harold J. Gibbons had a vision of a community that was fully integrated racially, socially, economically, and by age. With his influence and the support of progressive business-people, Laclede Town was built as an integrated neighborhood of 655 townhouses for middle-income families. The high-rise Heritage House for retired teachers and the Teamsters Council Plaza housing for the elderly were nearby. For years, the area was alive with art shows, theater, and music. But things turned sour, and by the late 1970s, Laclede Town was riddled with drugs and violence. Middle-class families moved out, and the townhouses were razed in the 1980s.

HERMANN STADIUM

Robert R. Hermann is one of the city's most enthusiastic boosters, and his generosity touches virtually every St. Louis institution. One of his greatest enthusiasms is soccer. In 1966, he helped form the National Professional Soccer League, which morphed into the North American Soccer League and has been replaced by Major League Soccer. The award for outstanding collegiate soccer players in NCAA Division I was named the Hermann Trophy in his honor.

The 6,000-seat Robert R. Hermann Soccer Stadium, built on the site of Laclede Town, is part of Saint Louis University. It has hosted six conference tournaments and has been an NCAA Tournament venue seven times. The field is not an elementary playing surface—the drainage system can filter ten inches of rain in an hour. During dry periods, a sprinkler system keeps the unique bluegrass mixture green no matter how many feet are running over it.

Fans crowd the stands for a night game at Robert R. Hermann Soccer Stadium at Saint Louis University.

HARRIS-STOWE STATE UNIVERSITY

The first St. Louis public school opened its doors in 1838; by 1860, the city had 23 elementary schools and two high schools. Central High (1855) was the first public high school west of the Mississippi for white students; Sumner High School (1875) was the first public high school west of the Mississippi for black students. Segregation in education was rigidly enforced until the Supreme Court decision in 1954 declared it unconstitutional.

In 1876, philosopher William Torry Harris became St. Louis schools' Superintendent of Instruction. He expanded the curriculum, added natural sciences and phonetic reading, and made it the most innovative system in the nation. About the same time, Susan Blow founded the first public kindergarten in a Carondelet school. With their child-size furniture, art materials, and educational games, kindergartens spread throughout the city and the United States.

An all-white teachers college was established as part of the St. Louis public school system in 1857 to supply classroom instructors. An all-black teachers school followed in 1890, also backed by the public school system. The white college was eventually named for Harris and the black one for author Harriet Beecher Stowe. The two colleges merged in 1955 as the school system began integrating and in 1979, became Harris-Stowe Teachers College. Today it is a state university, offering degrees in a variety of subjects but still focusing on educating educators.

Students enjoy fresh air at Harris-Stowe College in 1958, after the Harris and Stowe schools were integrated.

On Campus at Harris-Stowe

The Administration Building of Harris-Stowe State University is the flagship of the campus today *(above)*. It houses classrooms and many university-related offices, including the Office of the President of the university. It also contains the Don and Heide Wolff Jazz Institute, a privately owned jazz collection. Students can gather in the Hornet Dining Hall and Dining Annex for meals, much like they congregated in Harris-Stowe's college cafeteria in 1956 *(left)*.

SAINT LOUIS UNIVERSITY

One of Saint Louis University's treasures is its Vatican film library. During World War II, when Italy was a major battleground, Father Lowrie Daly, an archivist at SLU's library, became concerned about the danger to the Vatican library. Following the war, he persuaded Pope Pius XII to allow all documents in the library to be microfilmed for storage at SLU, and the Knights of Columbus agreed to provide the financing. The only cameras capable of handling such a huge job at that time belonged to the U.S. Air Force. Using them required an order from the commander in chief; SLU president Father Paul Reinert telephoned the White House. In short order, President Harry Truman agreed that the establishment of a Vatican collection in St. Louis would be a valuable addition to Missouri culture—besides, his nephew had done graduate work at SLU. The executive order was signed, and the cameras were sent to Rome. Between 1951 and 1957, some 12 million manuscript pages were captured on microfilm. Since then, thousands of manuscripts in dozens of languages have been added with ever more sophisticated equipment. These manuscripts attract scholars from throughout the world.

DuBourg Hall, shown here in 1935, was named for Bishop Louis William DuBourg. It was designed as a multipurpose building and contained a museum, classrooms, social student rooms, and elegant faculty and guest areas. Today, it houses SLU's administrative offices.

The SLU Scene

Today, students are always seen milling about SLU's campus *(right)*. St. Francis Xavier College Church (shown above next to DuBourg Hall) is also a gathering spot. In addition to masses and ministries, the "College Church" has space available for wedding receptions, dinners, and theater productions. The Xavier Grand Ballroom can hold up to 550 people.

CUPPLES HOUSE

Like Henry Shaw, Samuel Cupples arrived in St. Louis as a teenager, eager to make his fortune. He, too, sold goods to westward immigrants, becoming the largest woodenware distributor in the nation. He teamed up with Robert and Harry Brookings in 1866, and the Cupples firm diversified, meeting success with more success. In the early 1880s, Robert Brookings had a virtuoso idea: develop a warehouse district connected to the railroads, eliminating the need for drayage. In 1891, Cupples Station was born in the shadow of Union Station. At its peak, the Cupples Station complex—consisting of ten fireproof, architecturally acclaimed, seven-story warehouses—was handling 1,000 tons of merchandise every day. Hydraulic lifts transferred goods from the warehouse floors to track level. Cupples employees controlled the loading and unloading of goods, plus the scheduling of shipments, and it all worked like clockwork.

In 1888, Samuel Cupples hired architect Thomas Annan to build his home; it was ready for the family to move in two years later. The 42-room Romanesque mansion has Tiffany-style windows that diffract the sunlight. The interior wood carvings, done by English artisans, are in the geometric forms of the Arts and Crafts movement that was popular at that time. Cupples's Anglo-Irish heritage is reflected in Celtic design elements. After Cupples died in 1912, the Railroad and Telegraphers Union bought the house. They sold it almost unchanged to Saint Louis University in 1946. In 1973, Father Maurice McNamee began a meticulous restoration of the house, and today its elegance is unmatched.

The finished Cupples House in 1890 was built with purple sandstone from Colorado, laid on top of pink foundation granite from southern Missouri.

Intricate Design, Inside and Out

Today, Cupples House is on the campus of Saint Louis University and was placed on the National Register of Historic Places in 1976. Its lower floor houses an art gallery with collections of American and European paintings, as well as Christian art and iconography.

The first and second floors of the house are open to scheduled events; the university uses them to hold awards ceremonies, musical evenings, academic get-togethers, and other gatherings.

NORTH GRAND BOULEVARD

The first theater to open on North Grand was a vaudeville house, named The Princess Theater, in 1912. The million-dollar Missouri Theater opened in 1921 and became the home of the Missouri Rockettes, a precision chorus line. The Sun Theater, north of Powell Symphony Hall, was once Liberty Burlesque. Today, the Sun is still there, although boarded up; the others are gone.

Now, each year, North Grand Boulevard plays host to First Night. Invented in 2001 as a way to spend a safe, alcohol-free New Year's Eve, the area is blocked off for exhibits, performances, food, and fireworks. The weather has ranged from cold to very cold, but the crowds bundle up and come to celebrate anyway.

North Grand Boulevard was one of the liveliest streets in town during the 1930s and 1940s.

Left: In 1940, the parade escorting the Mystic Order of the Veiled Prophet of the Enchanted Realm traveled along Grand Boulevard on the way to select the Queen of Love and Beauty. The Veiled Prophet parade today travels down 4th and Market streets, ending at Union Station. Every year, it kicks off the Independence Day celebration at Fair St. Louis. *Below:* North Grand Boulevard has fewer theaters today.

ST. LOUIS THEATER/ POWELL SYMPHONY HALL

The St. Louis Theater, built in 1925 as a vaudeville venue, was part of the top-notch Orpheum circuit. Vaudeville, unlike burlesque, was family fare with fast-moving variety acts. Although still popular in 1925, vaudeville was on its way out. There were already 102 motion picture houses in the area by then. Movie houses were cheaper and easier to operate, and Americans loved the glitter of Hollywood. RKO took over the theater and converted it to a movie house. Like many theaters, the St. Louis struggled through the Great Depression, closing for months at a time until 1936. The 1940s and 1950s were good years for the Grand White Way, but with the 1960s, the exodus to newer outlying theaters began. The St. Louis Theater's last movie, a very successful one, was *The Sound of Music* in 1965.

In 1964, the Saint Louis Symphony Orchestra, then playing regularly at Kiel Opera House, was displaced by a convention and forced to find a temporary space. It tried the St. Louis Theater and found the acoustics there nearly perfect. Two years later it decided to buy the theater and renovate it, renaming it Powell Symphony Hall to honor a large donor. The Saint Louis Symphony Orchestra, founded in 1880, is the second-oldest professional orchestra in the nation and one of the city's greatest assets.

In the 1930s, the air-conditioned St. Louis Theater was a great place to spend a hot summer afternoon with Carole Lombard and Clark Gable. Uniformed ushers stand ready for the crowds.

Saint Louis Symphony's Permanent Home

Powell Symphony Hall was named for Walter S. Powell, an executive in shoe manufacturing; the Symphony Society was a beneficiary of a $1 million trust from his widow, Helen Lamb Powell. During renovation, the Symphony enlisted renowned acoustic engineer Dr. Cyril Harris to oversee the acoustical reconstruction, giving the Saint Louis Symphony Orchestra the ideal place to showcase its talents both in 1968 *(left)* and today *(above)*.

THE FABULOUS FOX THEATRE

Opulent. Lavish. Magnificent. The Fox Theatre takes one's breath away. Decorated in a style called "Siamese Byzantine," it is a mixture of Moorish, Thai, Indian, Egyptian, and anything else exotic and imposing. Built for $5 million, the 5,000-seat Fox opened on January 31, 1929, as the second-largest theater in the United States. Delighted theatergoers marveled at the lobby's majestic columns, ancient cloisonné elephant, dazzling mirrors, grand staircase flanked by marble lions leading to the mezzanine, and huge chandelier. Before the show began, a large Wurlitzer theater organ rose in front of the stage in a spectacular blaze of light.

However, even the Fox was hurt by the rush to the suburbs in the 1960s. It limped along with B movies until 1978, when it closed and began to deteriorate. Mary and Leon Strauss rescued the theater in 1981 and gave it new life. The multimillion dollar restoration perfectly recreated the astounding original. State-of-the-art sound, lighting, and stage equipment were installed. For the glittering reopening, organist Stan Kann sat at the immense Wurlitzer, which rose to thunderous applause. Today, the Fabulous Fox presents hit Broadway shows and other crowd-pleasing acts, and there are rarely any empty seats.

On the Fox Theatre's opening day in 1929, it presented the silent film *Street Angel*. The film's star, Janet Gaynor, later won an Academy Award for her performance.

Looking Fabulous Today

The Fox Theatre was opened by William Fox, founder of the Fox Film Corporation and the Fox West Coast Theaters. In 1927, a multitude of people were employed to build and design the Fox; construction crews, artisans, and craftsmen, along with architect C. Howard Crane, were responsible for the lavish interior. When Mary Strauss, a St. Louis arts philanthropist, convinced her husband, Leon, a real estate developer, to restore the theater in 1981, she wanted the renovation to closely resemble the theater's 1929 splendor. Some features had to be updated, such as new sound and lighting systems, but the rococo interior (shown above) enhances the experience of theatergoing. Today, the Fox Theatre patrons line up to see magicians, musicians, and musicals. Visitors can also stop by Peacock Alley—the fourth level of the theater that contains an exhibit celebrating the thousands of shows and stars that have appeared at the Fabulous Fox since 1982.

MIDTOWN

An aerial photo captures the life of the area.

A Continental Life Insurance Building (1929)

B Sheldon Hall (1912)

C Saint Louis University Museum of Art (1900)

D Masonic Temple (1926)

E Coronado Hotel (1926)

F Jesuit Hall, former Melbourne Hotel (1923, annex added 1929)

G Woolworth Building (1933)

H Pulitzer Foundation for the Arts (2001) and Contemporary Art Museum (2003)

I Scottish Rite Masonic Temple (1929)

The Saint Louis University Campus:

J Pius Library

K St. Francis Xavier College Church

L Verhaegen Hall

M DuBourg Hall

N Busch Student Center

The Continental Life Insurance Building first opened on the eve of the Great Depression. After standing vacant since 1979, it reopened in 2002, totally renovated with offices and luxury apartments.

Designed by Henry Switzer, DuBourg Hall, shown here in the early 1940s, was meant to be a modified Gothic style building.

The Many Faces of Midtown

Sheldon Hall (*above*) was designed by architect Louis C. Spiering, who also designed the 1904 World's Fair. Built in 1912 as the home of the Ethical Society of St. Louis, it became a music venue in 1964 when the Ethical Society relocated to St. Louis County. The building now houses a concert hall and art galleries and strives to provide diverse concerts, exhibits, and educational programs. Pythian Hall, another Midtown building, played host to the Knights of Pythias, a national fraternal organization. One of the organizations' St. Louis lodges (chapters) met in Pythian Hall in 1930 (shown at right). This building and its site later became the home of Carter Carburetor, which went out of business in the early 1990s.

Above: From 1900 to 1925, this French Renaissance building was the home of the St. Louis Club, an exclusive social organization that was the center of St. Louis social life. Several U.S. presidents visited the club, including presidents Roosevelt, Taft, and Wilson. The idea of the 1904 World's Fair was said to have materialized at the St. Louis Club. After a fire, the building was sold and used by various businesses over the years. Today, it's the Saint Louis University Museum of Art.
Right: Located across the street from Saint Louis University, the Masonic Temple is a distinguished presence on Lindell Boulevard. It holds meetings for members of the Grand Lodge of Missouri. The classic-style building has three receding stages, which are symbolic of the three steps in Masonry, and it contains beautiful stained glass and handcrafted furniture.

GASLIGHT SQUARE

In the early 1950s, the Beat Generation broke with traditional art and literature. From San Francisco to Greenwich Village, beatniks read their poetry and expounded on their philosophy in coffeehouses. In St. Louis, the "beat" area was at Olive and Boyle streets. Over the next 15 years, coffeehouses grew into nightclubs, bars, and restaurants. Jazz and bebop spilled out into the street. Beat Generation writers Jack Kerouac and Allen Ginsberg stopped at Gaslight Square, and some of the entertainers who performed there include The Smothers Brothers, Lenny Bruce, Miles Davis, Barbra Streisand, Jackie Mason, Mike Nichols and Elaine May, Woody Allen, Dick Gregory, Jack E. Leonard, and Webster Groves resident Phyllis Diller.

Urban decay in the surrounding area, the spread of illegal drugs, and the fear of crime led to the death of Gaslight Square in the early 1970s. Today's residential Gaslight Square exudes stability and decency.

Gaslight Square was built with the theme of the riverboat era in mind. The area was known for its elaborate Victorian style and, of course, gaslights.

From Nightclubs to Neighborhoods

A big part of the nighttime scene, a Dixieland band was a favorite crowd-pleaser for people sitting in sidewalk cafes or just strolling through the square in 1964 *(left)*. Today, the area has been redeveloped with new housing; Gaslight Square is a homey neighborhood now *(below)*.

A Good Place to Call Home

On the morning of May 26, 1780, several French inhabitants and their African slaves were working in their newly planted fields near the Grand Prairie, north of St. Louis. In Illinois country, across the Mississippi River, George Rogers Clark and a band of American rebels were engaged in a war with the British for independence from the crown. France had long supported American independence; Spain had recently declared war on Great Britain. British forces hoped to conquer both the Spanish and the French in St. Louis, and they relied on Sac and Fox Native American warriors for aid.

But the French were alerted months before the attack, giving Lieutenant Governor Fernando de Leyba of Spain (St. Louis was a French settlement that was ceded to Spain), time to build fortifications and gather weapons. When some one thousand Native Americans attacked on that May morning, an alarm was sounded and residents rushed to their prearranged stations (women were armed as well as men). Five cannons were fired and the Native Americans fell back, unwilling to die for the British. Accounts vary as to the number of St. Louisans who were killed or taken prisoner in the battle. It was probably about 100—a great loss for a town of 1,300.

Once independence was established and the Louisiana Territory was bought by the new United States, investors began checking out St. Louis for potential profits. New England Yankees arrived intending to create a mill town like the ones in the east. In 1816, three land developers incorporated the village of North St. Louis and platted the town using large circles (rather than the typical squared acreage) for a school, an assembly hall, and a church. Three main roads ran through the new village: the Great Trail (now North Broadway), which stretched from St. Louis to the Missouri River, Natural Bridge Road, and Florissant Road. Farther north, Hall's Ferry took passengers across the Missouri to Portage des Sioux.

BREMEN AND KERRY PATCH

About 25 years after North St. Louis was established, a trio of Germans founded the town Bremen (now part of the Hyde Park neighborhood). One of the founders, Emil Mallinckrodt, wrote enthusiastic letters home about the opportunities for buying cheap land north of St. Louis. Hundreds of families responded, and *Hallo dort!* and *auf Wiedersehen* replaced *allo!* and *au revoir*.

Shown here in 1890, Hyde Park was a peaceful place in which to spend time. It contained a bandstand, a greenhouse, and garden flower displays. Those features are gone today, but the park continues to be an area for community recreation.

Emil's three sons founded the Mallinckrodt Chemical Works to make agricultural chemicals for the surrounding rich farmland. The company later branched out into pharmaceuticals and industrial chemicals. During World War II, Mallinckrodt produced uranium compounds needed for the development of the atomic bomb.

The great Irish immigration began in the 1840s. So many people came to St. Louis from County Kerry that the area they settled around Cass Avenue was called Kerry Patch. Italians, Eastern European Jews, and African Americans eventually joined the Irish. It was a notoriously tough neighborhood with numerous gangs and frequent violent confrontations. Tenements were tightly packed with large families, and there was no sanitation system.

Most of those who lived on the north side, now called North City, regardless of nationality, worked in the grow-ing industries along the riverfront such as boatyards, lumberyards, brickyards, furniture factories, sawmills, sugar refineries, and glassmaking facilities. The brick buildings were utilitarian and usually adjacent to railroad tracks on one side and the municipal docks on the other. The "city beautiful" did not apply here.

CREATING A CULTURAL CENTER

Around 1858, a horticulturist named Charles M. Elleard bought a conservatory and greenhouses on farmland north of St. Louis. By 1870, the small town of Elleardsville, shortened to "the Ville," grew up around this property. Unlike many St. Louis neighborhoods, the Ville had no restrictive housing covenant. Middle-class African Americans found the area to be congenial and built scores of attractive houses and small businesses. Sumner High School, the first high school for black students west of the Mississippi, was established at 11th and Spruce streets

The Mallinckrodt brothers incorporated the family business in 1882. Their cluttered laboratory in 1890 held everything to help them prosper as agricultural chemical manufacturers. The brothers' contemporary, John F. Queeny, founded Monsanto Chemical Company. Monsanto is now known throughout the world for its agricultural technologies, and Mallinckrodt (operating within the healthcare products company Covidien today) provides pharmaceuticals and other products.

In May 2004, the Clark obelisk in Bellefontaine Cemetery was rededicated at the bicentennial of William Clark's journey west with Meriwether Lewis. A large gathering of Clark's descendants and leaders of the Osage nation were in attendance.

In 1941, the Cubs played the Cardinals in Sportsman's Park. Fans sitting behind homeplate could see the bleachers along the outfield and the massive scoreboard along the seats at left field. Once a recognizable North City spot, Sportsman's Park is now gone; the Cardinals play in Busch Stadium, downtown.

in 1875, but was relocated to the Ville in 1910. Other important institutions were established here as well, making the Ville "the cradle of black arts and culture" in the Midwest.

NORTH CITY LANDMARKS

As early as 1822, St. Louis was hosting agricultural and mechanical fairs. In 1855, an association of businessmen bought a 50-acre site for a permanent fair at Natural Bridge Road and Grand Boulevard. They added more acreage, an amphitheater, livestock stalls, a floral hall, and they landscaped it with fountains. During the Civil War, the Union Army took over the grounds and renamed it Benton Barracks. After the war, attendance at the fairs grew with the introduction of a horse show and sulky racing, consisting of lightweight, two-wheeled carts attached to both sides of a horse's harness, with the driver sitting right behind the horse. A zoo, an art gallery, and a natural history museum were also added. The fairgrounds served as the first home of the Veiled Prophet parade and ball, originally created as a Mardi Gras-like local celebration. In 1912, a five-acre swimming pool was built. But with the ascendancy of Forest Park, the fairgrounds dwindled in popularity. Today, it is merely a park.

The city's two largest cemeteries serve as the final resting place for city greats. Bellefontaine was established in 1849, the year of the cholera epidemic that took the lives of ten percent of the city's population. An average of 30 people per day were interred at the new cemetery during the epidemic. Next to Bellefontaine is Calvary, the 400-acre Catholic cemetery.

Completed in 1961, Highway 70 sliced through much of north St. Louis, destroying neighborhoods. Suburbia, too, claimed many one-time city residents. Hundreds of buildings were abandoned and left to decay or be demolished. Today, neighborhood associations, federal money, city organizations, and private investors are working together to rebuild North City. It is an area "in process."

COLUMBUS SQUARE

Columbus Square was once the roughest neighborhood in town. Gangs of tough Irish teenagers menaced Sicilians; Sicilians went after Poles and Russian Jews, who, in turn, fought back and chased down the Irish. Alley tenements nicknamed "Castle Thunder," "Clabber Alley," and "Wild Cat Chute" steamed in the summer, froze in the winter, and smelled all year round. Newly arrived immigrants could find cheap lodging there, and as many as five lived in the same room. Girls from the tenements worked in the garment trade or as maids; boys loaded freight on the docks, worked in the meatpacking plants, or became newsies selling newspapers on downtown corners. In response to the misery, social work grew through churches (St. Patrick's Catholic, St. Joseph's Catholic, and Grace Episcopal, which became Grace Hill Settlement House) and various charities for the ill, orphaned, and elderly, sponsored by John Mullanphy, a wealthy St. Louis merchant and philanthropist.

Above: Kids enjoy ice skating on a frozen pond in Columbus Square, on Carr and Biddle streets, in 1911. The rough-and-tumble tenements are in the background. *Left:* In 1864, the Shrine of St. Joseph was the site of a miraculous healing: A parishioner near death was restored to health after kissing a relic of Peter Claver. Jesuits dedicated an altar to St. Joseph in 1867 to show their gratitude for the city surviving yet another epidemic of cholera. Today, the Shrine of St. Joseph anchors the near North City neighborhood of Columbus Square.

CROWN CANDY KITCHEN

Crown Candy Kitchen was the perfect neighborhood hangout in the heart of Old North St. Louis. Kids had fun staring at the row of glass jars filled with candy, trying to decide where to spend their penny: a rope of licorice, a jawbreaker, maybe an all-day sucker. Teenagers loved the cozy booths, Frank Sinatra on the jukebox, and chocolate malts. Parents might shop at Marx Brothers Hardware or any of the other dozens of stores that lined St. Louis Avenue—perhaps even going as far north as Ed Schnuck's corner grocery or a kosher bakery—before stopping by Crown Candy for dessert. Nearby Maull's Spaghetti Factory made tons (literally) of pasta and the Meier and Pohlmann factory turned out furniture for Sears, Roebuck & Co. and Montgomery Ward.

Today, despite the abandonment of much of the neighborhood, Crown Candy Kitchen has only changed slightly since its opening in 1913 and is as popular as ever.

Harry Karandzieff and Pete Jagaloff brought their confectionery skills from Greece, opening Crown Candy Kitchen in 1913. Truly family owned and operated, Harry's son, George, took over in the 1950s, and today George's three sons run the shop. Crown Candy Kitchen prides itself on remaining the same year after year: The jukebox is always ready to play Teresa Brewer or Chubby Checker (right).

PRUITT-IGOE

Pruitt-Igoe is a textbook example of what not to do when it comes to housing complexes. In the mid-1950s, it seemed like the answer to low-cost urban housing. Architects and city planners applauded the 30 high-rise apartment buildings for their modern good looks and sanitization of poverty. Within 20 years, the complex had become a symbol of failure in urban housing.

In 1954, almost immediately after residents began moving in, it became obvious that the buildings were poorly designed and built with little regard for the people who lived there. The cheapest materials were used, especially in plumbing fixtures. Inexplicably, the elevators stopped only on every other floor. There were no playgrounds or teen centers for the great number of children,

nor were shopping facilities located nearby. Despite the best efforts of a tenants' association, no sense of community developed. Without the usual neighborhood controls, crime and violence soared. Residents moved out as soon as they could, and few people were willing to become new tenants. Vacant apartments were vandalized beyond repair.

Faced by so many irreparable problems, the city gave up. Pruitt-Igoe received national attention when the buildings were imploded between 1972 and 1975. Today, a public school, Gateway Institute of Technology, sits on part of the grounds of Pruitt-Igoe; the rest of the area is vacant.

Not even a 1968 clinic at the Pruitt-Igoe medical center was enough to build community spirit.

The Rise and Fall of Pruitt-Igoe

The modern high-rise Pruitt-Igoe complex seemed to be a good idea in 1956 *(above)*. Named for two St. Louisans, Wendell O. Pruitt, an African American World War II fighter pilot, and William L. Igoe, a former U.S. congressman, the building of the complex was an attempt to bring people back to the city after World War II. However, by the early 1970s, Pruitt-Igoe was deemed a failure, and the city's solution was to demolish it *(right)*, bringing national attention to the issue of public housing.

NEIGHBORHOOD GARDENS

Not all of the housing complexes built in the area were disasters. Neighborhood Gardens could be a model for livable, low-income housing. Around 1900, many St. Louisans became concerned about living conditions on the near north side. In 1908, the Civic League reported that 13,233 people lived in a 48-block area, primarily in substandard housing with no indoor plumbing. In 1911, residents, settlement workers, and a few altruistic souls who lived away from the community formed a neighborhood association, but little was done about living conditions until J. A. Wolf was appointed director. He spent four months studying low-cost housing in Europe and came back with a plan copied from Dutch and Austrian projects.

The result was Neighborhood Gardens, which opened in 1935. The 23 apartment buildings—each three stories—are grouped around four inner courtyards. Each apartment has a balcony overlooking greenery; 60 percent of the site is devoted to specifically designed and landscaped open space. There are no inner corridors; all apartments open directly from the stairs.

The simple, timeless design of Neighborhood Gardens, its clean brickwork and continued functionality, have put it on the National Register of Historic Places.

Recently, the apartments were renovated: bricks repaired, trash cleared, interior partitions built, and windows replaced. Neighborhood Gardens is once again an inviting site.

Neighborhood Gardens was the city's first low-income housing area in 1935. Playwright William Inge lived in the complex in the mid-1940s while teaching at Washington University.

FREIGHT DEPOTS

Between the end of the Civil War and the beginning of the Great Depression, railroads were responsible for much of America's prosperity. Because of its prime location, St. Louis was a major rail center with dozens of switching yards, freight warehouses, and freight depots.

Cotton was king in those years—a high-stakes business. Before the Civil War, the bulk of southern cotton went to New Orleans where it was shipped east. St. Louis wanted a piece of the pie and organized a Cotton Exchange that offered premiums to planters who would ship directly to the city. Promoters built large cotton compressors able to squeeze a 500-pound bale to the thickness of less than a foot—as many as 50 of these compressed bales could be loaded onto a single railroad car. In no time, St. Louis became the third largest cotton market in the nation, thanks in large part to the Cotton Belt Railway bringing unprocessed bales from Texas, Arkansas, and southern Missouri.

Above: For much of the 20th century, freight depots were scattered along the riverfront near manufacturers and warehouses, much like this one in the early 1900s. Twenty-two lines served St. Louis, including the Rock Island, St. Louis–San Francisco (Frisco), Chicago and Eastern Illinois (C&EI), Missouri–Kansas–Texas (Katy), and Missouri Pacific (MoPac) lines. Today, huge intermodal depots, such as those at Earth City, have replaced railroad freight depots. *Left:* The Cotton Belt Railroad Depot, built in 1911 when cotton was king, is now derelict.

GRAND AVENUE WATER TOWER

The Grand Water Tower at the center of the intersection of Grand Avenue and 20th Street is a longtime North City landmark. Called a perfect Corinthian column, it is 154 feet tall. The tower was built in 1871 to equalize the water pressure in the uncertain city water service. A companion water tower, 206 feet tall, was erected at Bissell and Blair streets in 1887. Neither has been used since 1912, and both have been placed on the National Register of Historic Buildings for their artistry.

In the late 1920s, lights were placed on top of the Grand Tower to serve as an aviation beacon, directing pilots to Lambert Field. The lights were turned off during World War II, as were all nighttime lights in that period of blackouts.

The Grand Water Tower stands in the center of a distressed area today. A neighborhood association called College Hill Community 2000 is determined to halt decay and reconstruct the community.

Top: Today, residents plant gardens in vacant North City lots for both beautification and produce.
Left: Shown here in 1958, the white Grand Avenue Water Tower and the red Bissell water tower are landmarks today. They are no longer used in the city's water system.

CHAIN OF ROCKS BRIDGE

The most distinctive feature of the old Chain of Rocks Bridge is one that woozy drivers feared and adventuresome ones looked forward to: the 30-degree curve in the middle. When a bridge between north St. Louis and Madison, Illinois, was first proposed in the 1920s, river pilots objected. A geological formation—a "chain of rocks"—made navigation difficult in that stretch of the river, plus they had to get around the city water intake towers. They would only agree to a bridge with a significant turn, allowing boats and barges to get by.

The bridge opened to traffic on July 20, 1929. In order to help pay the debt building it had incurred, tolls were charged—rather high for those Depression years: 35 cents for each car, plus 5 cents for each passenger. By the late 1950s, the toll had decreased to 15 cents per car. In 1936, the bridge was designated as a part of Route 66, bringing heavy traffic to the area. During World War II, the red sections of the bridge were painted green to provide camouflage from planes in the air. However, in 1967, two new bridges opened: the New Chain of Rocks Bridge to the north, and the Poplar Street Bridge downriver. Traffic on the old Chain of Rocks Bridge dwindled. When the aging bridge needed extensive repairs in 1968, the city of Madison decided to close it. An army demolition team planned to blow it up in 1975, but the profit from the resulting scrap was less than the cost of the demolition, so it was spared. In 1999, after two years of rehabbing, Trailnet turned the bridge into a pedestrian/cyclist corridor. Trailnet is a nonprofit, St. Louis-based organization that promotes walking and biking through the St. Louis region. Now the bridge links hikers and bikers to 300 miles of greenways and trails on both sides of the river.

Top: The bend in the Chain of Rocks Bridge is visible from the shore. Much of *Escape from New York* was filmed around the bridge. The 1981 movie starred Kurt Russell and was directed by John Carpenter. *Right:* Today the bridge, with Route 66 memorabilia, is part of the Trailnet cycling corridor.

Above and right: The Chain of Rocks Fun Fair amusement park was built in 1926 on a bluff overlooking the Mississippi. Its wooden Comet roller coaster was replaced by the popular Mad Mouse in 1959. The park burned in the late 1970s and has not been rebuilt.

Small boats traveling the stretch of the Mississippi called the "chain of rocks" must avoid boulders and snags to stay afloat. One of the city's water intake towers, built in 1894, can be seen in the background.

SPORTSMAN'S PARK

Sportsman's Park was built for the Browns in 1902. The St. Louis Cardinals joined them in 1920, and the two teams shared the park until the Browns left St. Louis for Baltimore in 1953—the same year that Gussie Busch bought the park and the Redbirds. The Brownies were loved by St. Louisans despite their dismal playing record. Astonishing the sports world, they won the American League pennant in 1944. The Cardinals, who were always on or near the top in those years, won the National League pennant the same year. Sportsman's Park was relatively small, seating only 30,500. During the historic streetcar World Series of 1944, when the whole city went baseball mad, the park overflowed with fans cheering for *both* teams. The Cards won the series in six games.

Reputedly, Sportsman's Park gave an advantage to left-handed power hitters, such as Stan Musial and Babe Ruth. Ruth hit three home runs at Sportsman's in the 1928 series, when the Yankees beat the Cardinals in four straight. The World Series of 1964 was a different story: Bob Gibson pitched an incredible 27 innings—three full games—with an ERA of 3.00, and the Cards won the series, beating the Yankees in seven games.

The last game played at Sportsman's Park (by then called Busch) took place on May 8, 1966. A helicopter carried home plate to the new Busch Stadium downtown. Shortly afterward, Sportsman's Park was demolished.

People pack the stands for a baseball game at Sportsman's Park at North Grand and Dodier.

A New Place to Play

After every Cardinal home run, the giant Budweiser eagle on the scoreboard flapped its wings while fans cheered, as shown above in 1969. Today, a part of this baseball diamond is incorporated into the Herbert Hoover Boys and Girls Club (HHBGC) playing field. Since 1967, HHBGC has occupied the site of Sportsman's Park *(right).* It provides youth from ages 6 to 18 with programs that deal with character, leadership, education, and career development; health and life skills; the arts; and sports, fitness, and recreation. HHBGC's wide-ranging sports program honors the tradition of Sportsman's Park.

CALVARY AND BELLEFONTAINE

Bellefontaine Cemetery was founded in 1849, just before the devastating cholera epidemic that claimed one in ten residents. Around 30 people died every day during that desperate time, and gravediggers worked around the clock. Cholera came back in the 1860s; in 1866, approximately 3,500 St. Louisans died from the disease during one summer. The deadly Spanish influenza arrived in the city in the fall of 1918 after it struck the East Coast (16,000 died in New York City in three weeks). Forewarned, Mayor Henry Kiel closed all schools, motion picture shows, billiard halls, cabarets, lodges, and other places where groups congregated until it seemed the epidemic had passed. In contrast with other cities, St. Louis lost fewer than 1,000 residents.

Bellefontaine is the final home of an interesting combination of St. Louisans: writer William S. Burroughs and poet Sara Teasdale; Confederate general Sterling Price and Union general Don C. Buell; engineers James B. Eads and J. S. McDonnell; brewer Adolphus Busch and cookbook writer and housewife Irma Rombauer, whose *The Joy of Cooking* is one of the all-time best sellers in the United States.

In 1858, Archbishop Peter Kenrick established the 400-acre Calvary Cemetery for Catholics next door to Bellefontaine. Buried here, among others, are Auguste Chouteau, General William T. Sherman, and Dr. Thomas A. Dooley, the founder of Medico, an international nonprofit medical care provider.

The gothic tomb of Adolphus and Lilly Anheuser Busch was built in 1915 at Bellefontaine Cemetery.

Prestigious Resting Places

Wealthy brewer Ellis Wainwright commissioned architect Louis Sullivan to design a tomb for his wife, Charlotte Dickson Wainwright. Sullivan, who also designed the Wainwright Building, is known for creating the skyscraper and mentoring Frank Lloyd Wright. The Wainwright Tomb *(left)*, a gray limestone cube topped by a dome, is decorated by a band of tulips along the top, sides, and over the door. The double-door entrance is surrounded by a snowflake design carved in stone. Another famous Bellefontaine plot is that of William Clark *(below)*. Settling in St. Louis after returning from his westward exploration, he served as governor of the Missouri Territory from 1813 to 1821, when Missouri became a state. He was then appointed superintendent of the Bureau of Indian Affairs. In all his dealings with Native Americans, Clark was considered honest and trustworthy. He died in 1838. The Clark memorial at Bellefontaine Cemetery pays tribute to his greatness.

FAIRGROUND PARK

Perhaps the most exciting St. Louis Fair occurred in 1860, when the Prince of Wales, the future King Edward VII of England, visited. More than 100,000 people turned out on a September day to see the prince admire prize cattle and ribbon-winning horses. The popular agricultural and mechanical fairs were more agricultural than mechanical, and the fairs waned in favor as the city became more urbanized. The last fair was held at the fairgrounds in 1902 and boasted the first automobile race in the city. The winner averaged a mind-boggling speed of 33 mph.

Fairground Park's worst day came in the summer of 1949, the day after Mayor Joseph Darst announced the mandatory racial integration of all city parks and pools. Fifty black children came to swim. They were met by 200 white teenage boys who told them they couldn't. A brawl ensued and several people were injured. To avoid more violence, Darst rescinded his integration order, but in 1950, the U.S. District Court ruled that the city must open all its park facilities to everyone.

Above: In 1896, the grandstand at Fairground Park held spectators for the horse races. *Right:* In 1912, the Fairground Park amphitheater was replaced by the first city swimming pool. In 1916, it was decided that the pool should be segregated by gender. An extremely unpopular decision, it didn't last. Shown here in 1938, men and women, boys and girls enjoy a dip.

A Park Transformed

A zoological garden was added to the Fairground in 1876. Modeled after European zoological buildings, the garden contained a monkey house, a carnivore house, and bear pits, with herbivorous animals and an aviary added later. The animals were moved to the zoo in Forest Park after the World's Fair of 1904. All other fair buildings were also removed. In 1958, the pool was redone and baseball diamonds and tennis courts were added. Today, Fairground Park is a recreational paradise, with playgrounds, fieldhouses, soccer and football fields, a basketball court, and a skating rink. Also, if park visitors are looking to do something a little more low-key, there are stocked lakes for fishing *(below)*. However, a piece of the old park remains—the castlelike entrance to the bear pits still stands at the corner of Grand and Natural Bridge *(right)*.

THE VILLE/ANNIE MALONE

Annie Malone was a brilliant businesswoman in a time when black women were generally relegated to servant status. Like other successful St. Louis entrepreneurs, she gave generously to the city. In the 1890s, Malone became interested in hair care and cosmetics for African American women. Within ten years, she had revolutionized the market and patented the first hot comb. She named her hair care products "Poro," a West African term for physical and spiritual growth. Her Poro College, established in the Ville in 1917, taught cosmetology. It employed nearly 200 people, and its building, which covered a whole city block and had a large roof garden, became a center for the rich African American culture of the Ville.

Around 1910, city teacher Sarah Newton saw a need for a St. Louis Colored Orphan's Home. The cornerstone of the home was laid in 1922, and the mortgage was burned in a jubilant ceremony less than 20 years later because of the generosity of its president, the millionaire Annie Malone. Today, the building houses the Annie Malone Children and Family Services Center.

The Ville Philanthropist

The Annie Malone Children's Home first opened as the St. Louis Colored Orphan's Home and occupied two other St. Louis locations before moving to Annie Malone Drive, which had been Goode Avenue *(above)*. In order to honor the contributions and good works of Annie Malone, the whole city participates in a parade for her each May *(left)*. Started around 1910 and shown here in the 1960s, the Annie Malone parade is still the center of the festivities during May Day. However, other events, such as live music and a Soiree dinner, are also part of the celebration that stretches over a weekend.

Above: The Annie Malone Children and Family Services Center today provides family reunification and parent education programs, along with emergency respite services and day care. It also houses Emerson Academy, a child development center. *Right:* This monument in the Ville commemorates the prominent people who came from the neighborhood, as well as the people and events that moved the city toward full equality.

HOMER G. PHILLIPS HOSPITAL

Homer Phillips was born in 1880 in Sedalia, Missouri, the son of a Methodist minister. As a young man, he became a civil rights advocate and turned to law, receiving a degree from Howard Law School in Washington, D.C., where he lived in the home of poet Paul Lawrence Dunbar and worked briefly at the Justice Department. He settled in St. Louis and became active in local politics, focusing on quality health care for African Americans. In 1920, more than 70,000 blacks lived in St. Louis, but just one 177-bed hospital attempted to serve them all.

Through Phillips's dogged efforts, a bond issue passed in 1923, and the new city hospital opened in the Ville in 1937, after his death. It was a first-class hospital that deserved all the superlatives given to it, from the well-designed exterior to the quality of care provided. As one of the few teaching hospitals anywhere open to black professionals, it trained a larger number of black doctors, nurses, X-ray technicians, lab technicians, and medical-record librarians than any other facility in the world.

In the late 1960s, the city began thinking of closing Homer G. for financial reasons. A long battle ensued, with its end coming in 1979. The hospital was abandoned, and all of its patients were sent to City Hospital.

Protests and demonstrations were held, but nothing could save Homer G. Phillips. Families even protested at the one-year closing anniversary, as shown here in a *St. Louis Globe-Democrat* photo from 1980.

Above: Today, the restored hospital is the Homer G. Phillips Senior Residence Center, with a healthy waiting list of would-be occupants. A nearby clinic serves the minor medical needs of residents. *Left:* After stalling the project for years, city officials were present for the hospital's opening in 1937.

SUMNER HIGH SCHOOL

The Missouri constitution of 1865 allowed for state support of black education. Ten years later, the first high school for black students opened in Missouri, named for Charles E. Sumner, the abolitionist senator from Massachusetts. Originally downtown, the school moved to the Ville in 1910. Since then, it has produced several generations of loyal alumni. Among its graduates are tennis champion Arthur Ashe; rock 'n' rollers Chuck Berry and Tina Turner; opera singers Grace Bumbry and Robert McFerrin; U.S. Representative William Clay; comedian Dick Gregory; TV anchor Julius Hunter; and former NAACP chair Margaret Bush Wilson.

World War II hero Wendell Pruitt, the Pruitt of Pruitt-Igoe housing, was also a Sumner alumnus.

The street running west of the high school is named for another graduate, Kenneth Billups, who, as a young music teacher in 1940, founded the Legend Singers. Dedicated to preserving and performing black folk music and spirituals, the Legend Singers have appeared at the Metropolitan Opera and with the Saint Louis Symphony Orchestra. Billups, himself a legend, became supervisor of music in the St. Louis Public Schools.

Sumner High School in 1950, when segregation was still a law in Missouri.

Above: Sumner High School today, in the heart of the Ville, has a mission to meet students' needs by providing a learning environment and helping them gain skills through technology, which will allow them to become effective members of, and contributors to, their society. *Left:* Sumner High School basketball coach John Algee and his players were jubilant after the Bulldogs defeated Webster Groves, 71–57, to win the Missouri Class L championship in 1969.

SCOTT JOPLIN HOUSE

Hearing a Scott Joplin rag conjured up the energy and excitement of a new 20th century. The free-flowing, syncopated rhythms seemed to underscore a brand-new era when musty, old traditions were on their way out.

Scott Joplin lived in St. Louis from 1885 to 1894 and again from 1900 to 1906. While in the city, he composed "The Entertainer," "Gladiolus Rag," "The Cascades" (for the World's Fair), and his opera *Treemonisha*. His most famous composition, "Maple Leaf Rag," was a sensation that opened the ears of middle-class whites to so-called Negro music. Fifty years after his death, Joplin's music was revived when "The Entertainer" was used in the hit movie *The Sting*. The St. Louis Legend Singers have performed *Treemonisha*.

The neighborhood association Jeff-Vander-Lou, Inc., purchased his house at 2658A Delmar as it was about to be demolished and, in 1984, donated it to the State of Missouri as a historic site.

The Scott Joplin house, in 1976, was in a state of disrepair before restoration.

SCOTT JOPLIN

Scott Joplin was born in Marshall, Texas, in 1868. By the age of 11, he was playing several musical instruments and improvising and composing his own music. He traveled throughout the Midwest as a teenager, playing the piano wherever he could, and received classical music training from the George R. Smith College for Negroes in Sedalia, Missouri. In St. Louis, in addition to his piano-playing at the Rosebud Café, he worked with the St. Louis Choral Symphony Society.

Above: Scott and his wife, Belle, lived in this house at 2658A Delmar from 1900 to 1903. During that time, it was in a blue-collar area with African Americans and German immigrants, close to the Chestnut Valley dive bars. It is now a Missouri Historic Site; it has been restored to its 1902 state and is open to the public. It contains museum exhibits dedicated to Joplin's life and music, as well as the New Rosebud Café, a reconstructed version of the bar and club where Joplin used to play. *Left:* Scott Joplin's 1907 "Searchlight Rag" is one of his lesser-known compositions.

The St. Louis Look

The Central West End was settled gradually and graciously. There were no families of immigrants crowding into flats without running water, no raucous sounds from manufacturing works, and no odors from downtown streets without sewers. From its inception in the mid-19th century, the area west of the city was developed as a place of beauty, elegance, and serenity.

To keep these neighborhoods chiefly their own—protected from those who were less affluent—residents created private streets. Downtown Lucas Place had been created as a private residential area early in the century, but with no buffer to keep the city from encroaching on it, residents moved away.

Julius Pitzman was responsible for most of St. Louis's successful private streets. Born in Halberstadt, Germany, in 1837, Pitzman arrived in St. Louis in 1854, bringing with him memories of parklike areas in Europe. He learned surveying while working for the city engineering department. His foresight and imagination led to the "St. Louis look" in affluent neighborhoods: massive stone and brick houses softened by landscaping, curved streets, boulevards, and most of all, space.

Private streets in the years before zoning allowed neighborhood associations to mandate deed restrictions: only single families of good character, primarily Protestant, English-speaking, and white. Traffic into private neighborhoods was carefully controlled. Lot size and minimum prices for houses were set. Residents paid the association for their own street lighting, sidewalks, and general maintenance.

WEALTHY PLACES

Between 1880 and 1920, many of the city's movers and shakers built large homes, bordering on ostentation, in Portland Place, Westmoreland Place, Hortense Place, Lenox Place, Westminster Place, and along Lindell Boulevard. For the most part, these people did not inherit wealth; they had used their entrepreneurial skill, business acumen, grit, and a hint of ruthlessness to make their fortunes. Many of them were philanthropists and patrons of the arts. They were also the people who gave St. Louis its tone: progressive in some ways, conservative in others—a mixture of noblesse oblige and Victorian rigidity.

The greatest buffer for those private neighborhoods was Forest Park, which the city established in 1876, almost two miles west of the city limits.

Forest Park offered many diversions, including a zoo, a history museum, and the Municipal Theatre. However, sailing model boats, as shown here, was also a popular pastime in the 1920s. The lakes were five feet deep and, through pipes, filled with water from the River Des Peres, Cabanne Spring, and storm water runoff. The water in the pipes was propelled by a steam pump and controlled by a valve system.

The Louisiana Purchase Exposition, otherwise known as the 1904 World's Fair, transformed Forest Park. Part of the park became an enchanted area of white palaces and lagoons, surrounded by artistic landscaping. The focal point was Festival Hall, designed by Cass Gilbert of New York, and the Cascade Gardens.

Plans for the beautifully wooded, 1,300-acre tract included carriage roads, lakes, and bridges. After streetcar lines reached the park in 1885, it became the most popular destination for city residents seeking recreation. In the 1890s, a gingerbread bandstand, a racecourse, and a restaurant were added.

Forest Park was a natural location for the 1904 Louisiana Purchase Exposition, the brainchild of David Francis and other city founders. Ironically, most of the beautiful trees in the western section were cleared for the "World's Fair." During the seven months of the fair, exotic foods, nightly light shows, unheard-of technology, exhibits in the 1,500 buildings, and performances from virtually every culture on earth dazzled 20 million visitors. After the fair, hundreds of trees were replanted in the park, and the elaborate landscaping seen today was begun.

The Highlands, another Central West End playground, opened in 1896 as a beer garden with family entertainment and a horse-drawn carousel. In 1905, the Japanese pagoda and a miniature train from the World's Fair were added. By the mid-1930s, the Highlands lured crowds with a ballroom, a huge swimming pool, picnic grounds, a penny arcade, and rides: a Ferris wheel, a roller coaster, giant swings, and a carousel. A fast-moving fire destroyed the Highlands in 1963. The carousel was rescued and moved to Forest Park.

The Jewel Box was built in Forest Park by the City of St. Louis in 1936. A conservatory with permanent floral displays, it has since been renovated to include a fountain, water feature, and a catering area. The space can be rented for wedding receptions, corporate meetings, and parties.

TAKING CARE OF RESIDENTS

At the urging of board president Robert Brookings, Washington University had opened a medical department for teaching physicians in 1894. At the same time, Robert Barnes, a wealthy banker who had arrived a penniless orphan in 1830, earmarked $850,000 from his estate to build a hospital open to all. Shrewd investments increased the fund to $2 million, and Barnes Hospital opened on Kingshighway in December 1914. Coincidentally, Washington University's School of Medicine moved to the same location at the same time. At its opening, Barnes Hospital had 250 beds and 26 patients. Four years later, the Spanish flu filled the hospital with patients, testing its ability to treat the sick. In 1919, Evarts Graham took over as head of surgery. A well-known pulmonary specialist, Graham was the first surgeon to successfully remove a lung. Very early he saw the connection between smoking and lung cancer. (A heavy smoker, he died of the disease in 1957.)

Children's Hospital, the oldest pediatric hospital west of the Mississippi, moved adjacent to Barnes in 1904, and Jewish Hospital joined them in 1927. The brand-new Jewish Hospital was declared the "Modern Hospital of the Year" for its innovations. Of the many research facilities that were built around the Barnes-Jewish complex, perhaps the most notorious was the Masters & Johnson Institute for Human Sexuality.

The Central West End (CWE) today buzzes with activity, accentuated by the hum of electric scooters belonging to residents of nearby apartments for people with disabilities. Restaurant row, along Euclid Avenue and its sidestreets, draws a wide range of foodies and music lovers. Nurses in hospital scrubs bump up against Sikhs; Segalese French come across Haitian French at Left Bank Books; the inclusive, diverse Trinity Episcopal Church offers tips on saving energy and the planet; Rothschild Antiques displays a Louis Philippe chest for only $3,500. All of these add to the unique CWE style.

CATHEDRAL BASILICA OF ST. LOUIS

Songs of praise and wonder come easily to worshippers inside the Cathedral Basilica of St. Louis, where they are surrounded by gleaming mosaics, marble, and gold leaf. A dozen artists from Ravenna Mosaics worked on the intricate designs, cutting the tesserae from sheets of glass and fitting them to follow the curvature of the domes. The murals covering the ceiling and walls took 80 years to complete and used more than 41.5 million pieces of glass in 7,000 colors. The artistry is breathtaking. The basilica itself is a distinctive synthesis of Byzantine and Romanesque design—solid and imposing.

On May 1, 1907, under the direction of Archbishop John J. Glennon, ground was broken for the new cathedral, closer to what was then the center of the city's population. Thousands of spectators crowded Lindell Boulevard to see the procession of the Holy Sacrament when the building was consecrated in 1926. Even more lined the streets when Pope John Paul II visited the city in 1999, hoping to get a glimpse of the pontiff in his "popemobile." During his stay in St. Louis, he participated in an ecumenical prayer service at the cathedral with Vice President Al Gore in attendance.

Archbishop Glennon's predeccessor, Archbishop John J. Kain, had been planning a new cathedral for some time. Setbacks occurred that consumed the archdiocesan funds, but Archbishop Kain wanted to see it through to the end—when he died, he left all of his personal estate to the cathedral building fund. The Cathedral Basilica, shown here in the 1930s, is rich in local history. The high altar was a gift from the McBride family, whose daughter was the first bride to be married in the new cathedral. The bronze gates of the Blessed Sacrament Chapel once decorated the Austrian exhibit of the 1904 World's Fair. The cathedral's lower level contains a museum that is dedicated to artifacts within the cathedral and follows the construction and installation of the mosaic tiles.

Inner Sanctity

The Cathedral Basilica's interior is a work of art *(right)*. At the far end of the sanctuary, the mosaics near the historic bay and dome honor the history of the Catholic church in the St. Louis area. The dome has the seal of the archdiocese. Moving to the middle of the sanctuary, the main dome—characterized by its bright red color—has four motifs. Finally, the arches of the cathedral are the Arch of Triumph, the Arch of Creation, the Arch of Sanctification, and the Arch of Judgment. The cathedral has been used frequently throughout the years, not just for masses but for weddings, baptisms, and RCIA (Rite of Christian Initiation of Adults). Below, Joseph Cardinal Ritter baptizes an infant in the cathedral in the 1960s. Three cardinals—John J. Glennon, Joseph Ritter, and John J. Carberry—and Archbishop John L. May are buried in the cathedral's crypt.

EUCLID AVENUE

From its earliest days, Euclid Avenue from Forest Park Parkway to Delmar Boulevard was a streetcar hub lined with shops, offices, and restaurants. Elegant dress shops, such as Saks Fifth Avenue, Montaldo's, and Peck & Peck, clustered around the Maryland and Euclid intersection. Long a landmark on Euclid was The Woman's Exchange, a tearoom that sold gift items made by women trying to support themselves and their families with their handiwork. Founded in 1883, the goal of The Woman's Exchange was (and still is) to provide opportunities for women with limited resources.

In the mid-1970s, the Euclid area started to decline, and many of the businesses moved out. The determination of local residents kept it alive; by the early-1980s, with a new set of tenants, the area was again vibrant.

Top: Euclid Avenue was lined with offices and shops in 1979. *Right:* Today, sidewalk cafes predominate the area.

HOLY CORNERS

Four religious institutions made their home at the intersection of Kingshighway and Washington Boulevard—the area that became known as Holy Corners. St. John's Methodist Church, built in 1902, was first. The First Church of Christ Scientist followed in 1904. Its congregation was organized in 1894 and was one of the first Christian Science churches in the United States. The Second Baptist Church, an offshoot of the church founded by pioneer minister John Mason Peck in 1833, moved to the location in 1907. Temple Israel also arrived in 1907; its congregation split off from Shaare Emeth. It was St. Louis's first Reformed Jewish congregation and was made up primarily of liberal German Jews. Holy Corners exhibited an extraordinary ecumenism for the time. Fellowship dinners, led by Methodist Bishop Ivan Holt, Rabbi Ferdinand Isserman, and the Rev. Ashby Jones, helped to break down barriers between Christians and Jews.

Holy Corners hasn't changed much over the years. The fifth churchlike building at Holy Corners is the Tuscan Masonic Temple, shown on the left, which recently celebrated its 5,000th meeting at that site. It stands next to St. John's United Methodist Church. The former Temple Israel is to the right of St. John's. In 1962, its congregation moved west to St. Louis County. The building and its educational annex were then used by a public high school for years.

CHASE-PARK PLAZA

Originally two elegant hotels, the nine-story Chase (1922) and the 27-story Park Plaza (1929) were connected in 1957. They, plus the Forest Park Hotel and several other hotels and luxury apartment buildings, were the domain of the Koplar family. Harold Koplar created an oasis of chic in the Chase-Park Plaza from the 1940s through the 1970s, with restaurants such as the Zodiac Room, the Sea Chase, and the Starlight Roof (with a skylight allowing diners to dance under the stars). The Khorassan Room played host to the Veiled Prophet and a few thousand of his friends for a dinner once a year. Jimmy Dorsey, Ray Anthony, Nat King Cole, Buddy Moreno, Milton Berle—all the great entertainers played at the Chase-Park Plaza, and all the visiting celebrities stayed there, from Eleanor Roosevelt to Elvis Presley, LBJ, and Sandy Koufax.

Professional wrestling came to the Chase in 1959, a few years after the Koplar TV station, KPLR (Channel 11), began to broadcast from its Videocruiser. Joe Garagiola was the first ring announcer. Harry Fender created his Captain 11 character for KPLR, thrilling a generation of children who came to the hotel studio for the show.

Harold Koplar sold the Chase-Park Plaza in 1981. Vacant for many years, it has been completely refurbished and is once again open for luxury living.

Above: In 1936, the luxurious Chase Hotel was home to the Chase Club, where patrons could see entertainers such as Bob Hope. *Left:* The Park Plaza was a favorite place for St. Louisans to celebrate all of life's milestones. This photo shows diners celebrating in 1932.

Today, the Chase-Park Plaza towers over Forest Park.

BARNES-JEWISH HOSPITAL

An epidemic of encephalitis hit the city in the blistering summer of 1933. More than 1,000 residents were afflicted—20 percent died. No one knew how the disease was communicated or how to stop its spread. The labs at Barnes Hospital became the headquarters for a team of investigators from the U.S. Public Health Department and researchers from Washington University Medical School. Many theories were advanced—it might be passed through milk or water or perhaps person-to-person contact. In an atmosphere of fear, the opening of school was postponed, and residents avoided crowded areas. Right before the first frost, researchers discovered that St. Louis encephalitis was caused by a virus; two years later, the culprit was located: the culex mosquito. The disease was not contagious.

In January 1996, Barnes and Jewish Hospitals merged to form Barnes-Jewish Hospital. Since then, Barnes-Jewish—along with its partners, Children's Hospital and Mallinckrodt Institute of Radiology—has been at the forefront of scientific medicine. Innovation has followed innovation in transplants, microsurgery, and genetic manipulation. The Siteman Center for Advanced Medicine employs 350 scientist-physicians who are aggressively attacking cancer with the same determination that earlier scientists had when searching for the cause of St. Louis encephalitis.

Above: Barnes Hospital opened in 1914, under contract to be a teaching hospital for the Washington University School of Medicine. Throughout its history, it was known for excellent patient care and advanced treatment. *Left:* Dr. Vilray P. Blair's plastic surgery amphitheater at Barnes Hospital in 1932 was decorated to distract patients and keep their minds off the operation. Blair pioneered reconstructive surgery of the face after trauma.

Barnes Hospital and the Jewish Hospital of St. Louis joined with Christian Health Services in 1993 to form BJC Health Systems. The giant BJC Medical Center draws patients from throughout the world. The nearby Center of Research, Technology and Entrepreneurial Exchange (CORTEX) is a hotbed for the development of high-tech medicine.

Left: General Henry C. Corbin, an architect of the Spanish-American War, led the parade for the dedication of the World's Fair in April 1904. *Below:* The Ferris wheel was designed for the 1893 World's Columbian Exposition in Chicago; a similar wheel was greatly popular at the 1904 Fair in St. Louis. Its 250-foot diameter made it the largest Ferris wheel in the world.

WORLD'S FAIR

The 1904 World's Fair, or Louisiana Purchase Exposition, is still one of St. Louis's fondest memories. It was an enormous operation involving thousands of people and years of planning. In August 1901, President William McKinley issued a proclamation inviting all the nations of the earth to participate in the exposition. Most of them agreed to do so, an amazing response in that era of little communication among cultures. Exhibitors from Togo to Thailand, Belgium to Brazil brought the best aspects of their respective nations to St. Louis for everyone to admire. The setting was perfect, with elaborate gardens, cascades, lagoons, and magnificent (albeit temporary) buildings; the once-in-a-lifetime experience drew millions of visitors.

Putting the park back together after the fair closed in November 1904 took years of grading, terracing, and replanting and caused quite a bit of controversy. Should the park be returned to its natural state, or should it continue to be developed into a community-gathering place? The developers prevailed, leaving only a small section in the southwest corner of the park as wilderness. With the surplus money from the exposition, the promoters built a World's Fair Pavilion with comfort stations, a refreshment bar, and space for events.

Above: The World's Fair Pavilion was built in 1909 with proceeds from the 1904 World's Fair. It was renovated in 1998, and today, looking out over Forest Park, it offers a scenic setting for all sorts of events from private receptions to company picnics. *Right:* The movie *Meet Me in St. Louis* was released in 1944, during the grim days of World War II. It became an instant classic for its portrayal of a safe, happy time with lovable characters who lived in St. Louis during the World's Fair. Screen favorites Judy Garland, Mary Astor, and Margaret O'Brien starred in the film, which was based on the short stories of Sally Benson, who lived in north St. Louis at the turn of the 20th century. *Far right:* A colorful postcard showing the Blanke Aerial Globe was used to promote the World's Fair in 1904.

The 1914 Pageant and Masque of St. Louis celebration used Art Hill as an open-air theater.

THE PAGEANT AND MASQUE AND THE MUNY

Civic reformer Charlotte Rumbold hoped to bring the disparate popula- tions of St. Louis together in a grand "Pageant and Masque" that would tell the history of St. Louis on an epic scale. With the Civil League's backing, the pageant, involving thousands of actors, singers, costumers, and stagehands, was performed at the bottom of Art Hill in Forest Park from May 28 through June 1, 1914.

A gigantic mound built on stage introduced the mound builders; individ- uals representing Cahokia, the Mississippi River, St. Louis, the Pioneer, War, Poverty, Gold, Beauty, and Love also made their entrances and exits. The story told of the triumph of good over evil and the power of progress. A half-million people applauded its message of civic pride.

The popularity of the Pageant and Masque and other dramas held in the park, such as the 1916 production of Shakespeare's *As You Like It*,

convinced city officials that outdoor theater belonged in Forest Park. The original idea was to present grand opera, and the name chosen for the endeavor was the Municipal Opera. A permanent outdoor theater with 10,000 seats was built in 1917 and called the Municipal Theatre (short- ened to the Muny); *Aida* was the first opera staged, followed by *I Pa- gliacci* and *Carmen*. Out-of-town professionals were hired for the produc- tions; local actors, singers, and dancers made up the chorus—a tradition that has continued.

For a while, the garment and shoe manufacturers in town presented fash- ion shows for buyers on the Muny stage, and occasionally the Symphony Orchestra or popular bands offered an evening of music. Gradually the Muny moved into presenting musical comedy, the quintessential Ameri- can form of entertainment, and its thousands of enthusiastic patrons continue to give that choice a standing ovation.

The Magic of the Muny

The Muny was built from scratch in a little over six weeks and includes a huge stage and an orchestra pit for up to 200 musicians, as well as dressing rooms for performers. In 1918, tickets for Muny performances went for 25 cents to one dollar, but about 1,600 of the 9,000 seats were reserved as free. Today, ticket prices have gone up—for nine dollars a theatergoer can sit in terrace C, while $64 provides center or side box seats. However, the tradition of free seating still remains. Other things at the Muny have changed as well—the Muny now offers the Muny Kids and Muny Teens, a performance troupe whose members are determined by auditions. Youth aged 7 to 18 who are accepted are given a chance to spotlight their talent and gain perfomance training and experience. The Muny has put on many shows over the years, from its first performance of *Aida* to the more recent *High School Musical,* and St. Louisans, not put off by humidity, mosquitoes, or threatening thunderstorms, still fill the seats every summer.

ST. LOUIS ZOO

St. Louisans began collecting animals for a small zoological garden at the fairgrounds in the 1870s. When the area was sold in 1891, some of the animals were informally housed in Forest Park. In 1910, the St. Louis Zoological Society formed in earnest, but with no clear idea of how to build a zoo. Some members wanted range animals only—deer, bison, and llamas who would graze throughout the park. Mayor Henry Kiel stressed investing in exotic animals such as elephants, lions, tigers, and monkeys. A donor sent a kangaroo, and another sent a grizzly bear. Without proper facilities or care, the animals languished. In 1915, the state legislature authorized the establishment of a zoo, and marketing master George Vierheller became the director. His efforts turned a dispirited group of animals into a top attraction and mildly curious visitors into delighted zoo boosters who couldn't wait to come back.

The second zoo director was Marlin Perkins. A national celebrity through his popular *Zoo Parade* and *Wild Kingdom* television programs, Perkins urged respect for all animals, from garter snakes to hippos, and stressed the zoo's mission to teach science. Today, the St. Louis Zoo is one of the top zoos in the nation and a leader in preserving endangered species.

Phil the gorilla lived at the zoo from 1941 to 1958. He was much loved for his intelligence and good humor. After his death, he was mounted and placed back in his habitat. Here, zoo visitors in 1959 see him as he appeared in life. Phil is still there today.

Amongst the Animals

The St. Louis Zoo has come a long way from exhibiting animals in small cages *(above)*. Today, zoo animals live in an environment specifically designed to be as close as possible to their native habitats. For example, the ten-acre River's Edge immerses visitors in a river environment where hippos, rhinos, and elephants play. The Zooline railroad *(right)* was constructed in the early 1960s to provide visitors with a narrated tour of some of these habitats, along with favorite zoo exhibits. The St. Louis Zoo not only cares greatly about the welfare of its animals but the welfare of animals in other areas as well. In 2004, the Wild Care Institute was established, concentrating on 12 conservation centers around the globe. Its mission is to help create a sustainable future for wildlife around the world.

ART MUSEUM

An art museum affiliated with Washington University's fine arts department was established downtown in 1881. After the World's Fair, it moved into the Palace of Fine Arts building designed by Cass Gilbert. Most fair buildings were intended to be temporary and were made of "staff," a concoction of plaster, hair, and other organic fibers, but the building used to house art collections had to be fireproof, and thus was made of granite and marble. Gilbert chose the summit of a hill, the highest point in Forest Park, for his Beaux Arts–style building. An inscription on the museum reads, "dedicated to art and free for all."

The statue of a heroic St. Louis (King Louis IX of France) astride a horse, as seen on the facing page, also came as a result of the fair. Originally a small plaster statue, later it was enlarged and cast in bronze. A crowd of 25,000 cheered the unveiling of the statue on October 4, 1906, and it instantly became a symbol of the city.

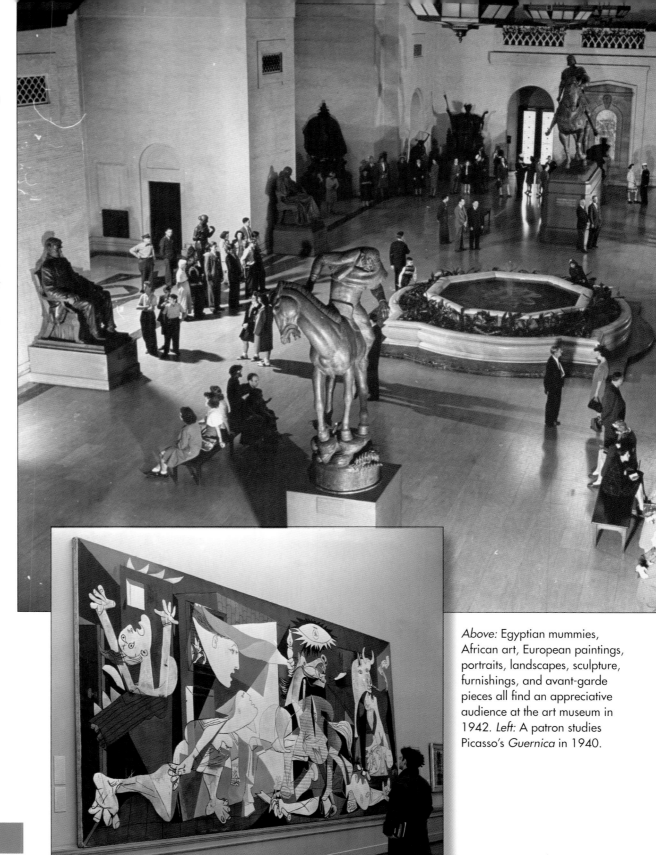

Above: Egyptian mummies, African art, European paintings, portraits, landscapes, sculpture, furnishings, and avant-garde pieces all find an appreciative audience at the art museum in 1942. *Left:* A patron studies Picasso's *Guernica* in 1940.

Featuring collections ranging from American and European art to decorative arts and design, the museum has free admission, giving everyone the chance to visit the galleries as often as they want throughout the year. In 2007, the Saint Louis Art Museum revealed plans to expand—the galleries and public spaces will increase in size to provide more space for touring exhibitions as well as the museum's own large collection. In addition to art collections and exhibitions, the museum contains The Richardson Memorial Library, which is a research center, and Puck's, a restaurant overlooking Sculpture Terrace. The statue of St. Louis watches over Forest Park from atop Art Hill in front of the art museum.

Left: People gather on the lawn during the 1980 Fourth of July celebration on Art Hill. A good place for gathering, Art Hill has been used for other festivities over the years, such as the Earth Day celebration in 2008. *Below:* An enormous crowd welcomed aviator Charles Lindbergh back to St. Louis in June 1927 after he flew alone across the Atlantic Ocean.

ART HILL

After the World's Fair, when the temporary buildings around the Palace of Fine Arts were cleared and the miniature train dismantled, the beauty of the slope of Art Hill became evident. Its broad openness made a natural amphitheater and it became the site of citywide celebrations. John Philip Sousa led his 350-man band there for a 1918 Liberty Loan rally. But perhaps the greatest celebration occurred on June 19, 1927, when Lindbergh returned.

The young Charles Lindbergh worked as an airmail pilot out of Lambert Field in the 1920s, flying the Chicago run. When he decided to try for the Orteig Prize, to be granted to the first aviator to fly across the Atlantic Ocean, he turned to nine air enthusiasts in St. Louis for backing. They came up with the funding, and, in gratitude, he named his biplane *Spirit of St. Louis.* Virtually every American with access to a newspaper or crystal radio set was thrilled by the news of his successful 33-hour flight from New York to Paris in May 1927.

After flying over the huge crowd at Art Hill several times, Lindbergh landed at Lambert Field and then flew back to Forest Park. There he placed a wreath on the statue of St. Louis and again proclaimed his appreciation for the city that believed in him.

Workers restoring Art Hill after the World's Fair discovered that it is perfect for sledding. As shown here in 1978, kids lined up to take their turn flying down the hill. It's still a very popular sledding hill today.

HISTORY MUSEUM
AND RIVER DES PERES

David Francis, chief organizer of the World's Fair, wanted a statue of Thomas Jefferson in Forest Park as a permanent testament to the greatness of the man. Jefferson, who was responsible for the Louisiana Purchase, had no monument in the United States at the time. On April 8, 1911, ground was broken for the construction of Jefferson Memorial at the north central entrance to Forest Park. A building was constructed around the statue to house the archives of the exposition and the collection of the Missouri Historical Society, which had been formed in 1866. Today, Karl Bitter's massive marble statue of Jefferson dominates the entry.

In 1883, when Forest Park was only a few years old, the River Des Peres that crossed the area was clear and sparkling, running with fish. By 1894, it was an open sewer poisoning the air and ground, a menace to health. The river's periodic floods left an unspeakable residue that turned people away from the park. Residential districts without city sewers had grown up north of the park and polluted the river beyond restitution. Some of the river's sewage was enclosed in pipes during the fair, a temporary solution. In 1923, a permanent solution was found, and the entire river was routed underground using huge, 29×23-foot pipes.

Top: River Des Peres means "River of Our Fathers," and was once a site for recreation for early St. Louisans. However, after flooding and sewage problems, residents were relieved when work began to route the river under Forest Park, as shown here in 1929. *Right: The Spirit of St. Louis* was named for Charles Lindbergh's St. Louis supporters, who paid for the plane. After returning from his solo flight, Lindbergh went on a three-month national tour, flying *The Spirit of St. Louis* to cities all over the country to promote aviation. A replica of the plane hangs in the History Museum; the original is in the Smithsonian National Air and Space Museum.

Missouri History Museum

Originally called the Jefferson Memorial Building, the Missouri History Museum was built using proceeds from the 1904 World's Fair and was the first national monument to President Thomas Jefferson *(above)*. Now managed by the Missouri Historical Society, the museum not only contains the Thomas Jefferson statue but also continuing exhibits on Charles Lindbergh and the 1904 World's Fair, as well as *Seeking St. Louis*, which explores St. Louis's past, present, and future. Today's interactive exhibits make learning the history of the city fun. Traveling exhibits make stops at the Missouri History Museum, too. The "Baseball as America" exhibit arrived in December 2004, drawing former St. Louis Cardinals shortstop and Baseball Hall of Fame member Ozzie Smith *(right)*.

Left: Boating in the Grand Basin was the rage in the 1890s. Today, the Grand Basin is still a scenic spot; several locations in the area are popular for wedding ceremonies. *Below:* A leapfrog race was part of the City Playground Festival in 1914.

FOREST PARK

From the beginning, Forest Park was intended to be a place to play. The Triple A (Amateur Athletic Association) was formed in 1897 and immediately built tennis courts, a baseball diamond, and a nine-hole golf course in the park. Bicyclists, walkers, runners, ice skaters, roller skaters, boaters, and equestrians have also enjoyed the park. Tobogganing, cricket, lacrosse, lawn tennis, croquet, handball, and basketball have had their participants as well.

Progressives thought that recreation should be democratic and unifying, with no sense of an exclusive, by-invitation-only atmosphere. African Americans were allowed in Forest Park but were usually segregated from whites until well into the 20th century.

In 2007, the Triple A golf course was redesigned and landscaped in 1920s style. The clay tennis courts were also upgraded. All the athletic facilities are well used in Forest Park, in fair weather or foul, whether by organized teams or individuals. It is a place in constant motion.

In addition to envisioning Forest Park as a giant athletic field, the planners also hoped it would be a retreat from the oppressive noise, pollution, heat, and other city stresses—a haven of tranquility. By 1930, it was less a refuge from the city and more a crowded recreation and education center, a civic gathering place with amusements for almost every taste.

The park was designed as a driving park, with roads that meander through it. Whether made up of carriages, bicycles, Model As, motorcycles, or SUVs, traffic was a problem from the beginning and continues to be so. In 1896, vehicles were fined $25 for not keeping to the right on roads. Mounted police and patrol cars have helped to create order in the constant parade of vehicles. They've kept an eye on parked cars as well; young lovers could expect a rap on the window and a flashlight shining in their eyes in the 1940s and 1950s. The most frustrating part of driving in the park is getting lost—almost everyone has done it at least once, despite the signs and arrows.

In the 1970s, the park began to deteriorate. A preservation group, Forest Park Forever, was organized in 1986. Using private and public money, it restored much of the park's beauty and tranquility.

Skaters have always loved Forest Park—Steinberg Skating Rink recently celebrated its 50th year there. In the winter, the rink fills with skaters of all ages. Open at night, many people come out to enjoy skating beneath the stars. During the summer months, the rink offers sand volleyball courts for league play.

Fun in Forest Park

Forest Park is still alive with activity today. People go boating on Post-Dispatch Lake *(left)*. In the background, the boathouse serves as the entrance to the lake. Boaters can go from the boathouse, through the lake, around two islands, and into the Grand Basin. The beauty of Forest Park also lends itself to weddings and walking tours, and it calls painters to their easels *(bottom left)*. If visitors come for sports, there are plenty of related leagues and clubs in which to participate. Forest Park is also home to the Dwight Davis Tennis Center *(bottom right)*. Tennis enthusiast Dwight Davis donated the Davis Cup as a prize for a men's tennis tournament, the Dwight Davis Championship, in 1900. It has become the largest international team competition in sports. Today, the center is open to the public, with tennis programs, tournaments, and events available to all. The St. Louis Aces also play to large crowds at the Dwight Davis Tennis Center.

Nikki Caplan and John O'Toole founded the Great Forest Park Balloon Race in 1973, and today it is one of the most popular one-day balloon races in the country. It launches in Forest Park, and attendance is free to the over 100,000 spectators who come to watch the balloon pilots compete. In May 2000, the Great Forest Park Balloon Race was made a part of the permanent collection of the Library of Congress.

An 1896 aerial view of the private streets of Westmoreland and Portland places.

WESTMORELAND AND PORTLAND PLACES

Westmoreland and Portland places were designed as a safe enclave for the wealthy. Tourists today marvel at the extraordinary architecture and landscaping of the neighborhood. The first residents earned their right to privacy, security, and beauty in the pre-tax, pre-regulatory agency days, mainly through creative entrepreneurship. They were the city's major employers in tobacco, railroads, steel, banking, hardware, shoe manufacture, and retail. Early Westmoreland and Portland homeowners were connected through the neighborhood, as well as business associations, clubs, civic projects, social events, and recreation. Most of them had a sense of civic pride and responsibility; their contributions of money and volunteer hours kept many St. Louis organizations and institutions alive.

Westmoreland Place today is a gated community.

Living in Luxury

Westmoreland and Portland places were founded in 1888 and designed by Julius Pitzman to provide a sense of beauty and stability. A mansion was the norm for the wealthy St. Louisans who lived at Westmoreland Place *(left)*. Children of the original owners of Westmoreland Place and Portland Place homes moved into similar communities at Lenox Place, built in the 1930s, just a mile away. The architecture today is still handsome and dignified; the landscaping graceful and fitting *(below)*. Everything about the neighborhood says refinement.

THE ARENA

In October 1929, Ben G. Brinkman, who had just bought The Highlands, opened a large exposition hall he called The Arena. Covering three acres with seating for 21,000, it offered more floor space than Madison Square Garden. Its unusual oblong dome was lamellate construction, designed for strength. In its first few months, The Arena hosted a national dairy show, a national horse school, and a Boy Scout circus. An ice rink large enough for ice shows and hockey games was added in 1931. During World War II, the space was used for glider assembly.

No matter how many expositions, political rallies, indoor soccer games, and concerts were held at The Arena, it was best known as the home of the Blues hockey team. The noise level soared when the Blues skated in and rarely lowered below a roar, sometimes drowning out broadcaster Dan Kelly. Ralston-Purina bought the Blues and The Arena in 1977, renaming it the Checkerdome. They sold both in 1983, and once again The Arena was known as The Arena. Growing more decrepit each year, it lasted until 1994 before it was closed. A dinosaur by 1999, it was imploded while hundreds of watching fans cringed and the echoes of Ernie Hays's inimitable organ music hung in the air.

The Arena, affectionately called "the old barn," played host not only to dairy shows, but also circuses and roller derby competitions. In the 1950s, it lost a tower in a violent storm. The other tower was pulled down to keep the building symmetrical.

The End of The Arena

The Eagles were the first major-league hockey team in 1934. Then came the Braves and the Blues. The St. Louis Hawks, Spirits, Billikens (basketball), and Steamers (indoor soccer) also used The Arena. The 1980 boxing match between Leonard and Duran took place in the renamed Checkerdome (*right*). In 1992, Bigfoot won the world championship of monster truck racing. The old barn was finally closed when the Blues moved to their new home in the Kiel Center. At the 1999 implosion (*above*), The Arena lasted about fifteen seconds after 133 pounds of TNT, placed in 250 spots, were ignited at once. When the dust cleared, all that was left was a pile of rubble and memories of concerts by Jethro Tull, Aerosmith, Bob Dylan, Led Zeppelin, the Beach Boys, Chicago, Alice Cooper, and Elton John.

CHECKERDOME

SOLD OUT LEONARD VS DURAN CLOSED CIRCUIT
JUNE 21 THE LITTLE RIVER BAND 8 PM
JUNE 21 EXHALL N.A.S.C.O. JAMBOREE SALE

Left: Before its demise in 1963, the Comet was purportedly the highest, longest, fastest, and grandest roller coaster in the nation. *Below:* The first roller coaster at the Highlands, in 1902, looks child-size.

FOREST PARK HIGHLANDS

Anton Steuver opened The Highlands in 1896 as a beer garden with family entertainment, which more than likely consisted of an oom-pah band. He soon added a horse-drawn carousel and a miniature train, and he brought over the Japanese pagoda from the World's Fair. The Highlands expanded through the 1920s and 1930s, adding a ballroom, a swimming pool, a fun house and penny arcade, and rides. It became a favorite spot for family picnics and school outings. On July 19, 1963, a fire started in the basement of The Highlands Restaurant. The place quickly emptied, and the wind whipped flames through the Flying Turns, the arcade building, the fun house, and the Ferris wheel, destroying everything except the carousel—even the beloved Comet roller coaster. TV personality Charlotte Peters happened to be broadcasting her show from The Highlands that afternoon and gave live coverage of the disaster.

ST. LOUIS COMMUNITY COLLEGE (STLCC)

Suffragist Anna Sneed Cairns opened the first Forest Park College in 1891, which offered a school of music, as well as high school and some college work. It was for women only, and it drew both boarding and day students. Parents felt their daughters were safe in the environs of the park and would benefit from the open air and beautiful scenery. The college closed in 1926 because of the ill health of Cairns, and the buildings were eventually demolished.

In 1967, St. Louis Community College at Forest Park opened on the approximate site of The Highlands. Its extensive campus serves thousands of students each year, offering both academic and applied education.

Expanding Minds, Changing Lives

The compact campus of St. Louis Community College at Forest Park belies its size. In addition to classrooms, the campus also contains a children's center, an art annex, and a performing arts center theater. STLCC offers several degrees and certificates, as well as continuing education classes and distance learning courses. It also has what it calls Workforce Development, which provides programs and services meant to prepare students, businesses, and organizations for the workplace.

WASHINGTON UNIVERSITY IN ST. LOUIS

Transplanted Yankees founded Washington University as Eliot Seminary, a nonsectarian college, in 1853. Named for its director, William Greenleaf Eliot, it was renamed for the nation's first president in 1857. It remained a small school of 100 mostly local students until Robert Brookings was appointed to the board in 1895. His vision and money propelled it toward its future as a major, first-class institution. Other university boosters, especially David Francis and Samuel Cupples, also contributed much in its early days. Chancellor Arthur Holly Compton, a Nobel Prize physicist, drew world-renowned scientists to the campus in the 1950s. Since then, 22 nobelists have been associated with the university.

Today, Washington University is known for its professional schools and institutes, especially the George Warren Brown School of Social Work, which is the nation's top-rated graduate school of its kind. The university has received national attention for hosting presidential and vice presidential debates during election years.

An aerial view of Washington University in 1947 shows Brookings Hall as the most prominent building on campus. The castlelike Brookings housed the administration for the 1904 World's Fair.

Today, students crowd the quad at Washington University during student activities fairs. The quad is enclosed by Brookings *(shown above)*, Ridgely, Cupples, and Busch halls.

County Culture

St. Louis County was organized in 1812, almost ten years before Missouri became a state. From the beginning, St. Louis County had a different feel from the city of St. Louis. It was settled by farmers and trappers from Virginia, Tennessee, and Kentucky who were wary of the city and its ethnic neighborhoods. These early county residents, in the manner of Daniel Boone, sought space; they were not looking to build a community.

In his 1911 *History of St. Louis County*, William Thomas wrote, "The pioneers were a sturdy, self-reliant, industrious, sagacious, most resourceful band [with] an abundant supply of initiative. They were, despite the privations, hardships, and savage environment, cheerful and contented, courteous, and courtly." Thomas reported that their slaves were happy as well. They all may have been cheerful and contented, but they had little cash and thus bartered, trading beeswax, whiskey, salt, wood, fish, and most of all, furs for the goods they needed.

The French who moved into Florissant contrasted with these robust, self-reliant American settlers. Founded in the late 18th century during Spanish rule, Florissant was originally named St. Ferdinand and was laid out in the style of a European city. The houses were built close together and had access to a common field. Nearby Spanish Lake also dates from the late 18th century. Originally called Spanish Pond, it was named for the troops who built Fort Carlos in 1768.

Immediately after the Louisiana Purchase in 1803, American soldiers constructed Belle Fontaine Cantonment at the confluence of the Missouri and Mississippi rivers. It was the first U.S. military post in the new territory, although it functioned more as a trading post for Native Americans. Meriwether Lewis and William Clark stayed overnight at the post on their return from the Corps of Discovery expedition.

SETTLING IN

As Americans began settling the frontier, soldiers were assigned to protect them. Along the Mississippi River south of St. Louis, the U.S. Army established Jefferson Barracks in 1826 as the nation's first "Infantry School of Practice." Over its lifetime, Jefferson Barracks was the headquarters for troops bound for the Mexican War, Civil War, various Native American conflicts, the Spanish-American War in Cuba, the war in the Philippines, World War I, and World War II. It also housed the first Army Air Corps basic training site. Jefferson Barracks was closed in 1946—it is now a historic park.

The stable at Jefferson Barracks, built in 1851, was home to four horses that hauled wagonloads of munitions from the St. Louis Arsenal to the various ordnance magazines in Jefferson Barracks. The stable was unusual in that it had a front and back door, allowing two teams to pull in simultaneously. The arsenal was moved to the barracks in 1871; the arsenal grounds became Lyon Park, at Broadway and Arsenal Street. The stable is still present today, in what is now Jefferson Barracks County Park.

E. G. Lewis, the founder of University City, commissioned the Lion Gates (also referred to as the Gates of Opportunity) in 1909. There are actually two pillars, one with a lion and one with a lioness; only the lioness pillar is shown in this photo from the 1920s. Sculptor George Julian Zolnay constructed the lion and lioness of concrete, and each weighed eight tons. They originally stood atop 40-foot pylons of limestone. Over the years the pylons began to lean. In 1991, they were shortened to 14 feet, and the concrete lions were replaced with lighter fiberglass models. The original lions are in the collection of the Missouri Historical Society.

By 1850, Missouri was eager to build railroads. Completion of the first and second divisions of the Missouri Pacific, in 1853 and 1855 respectively, simplified the commute from the county to the city and spurred the building of bedroom communities: Kirkwood, Webster Groves, Valley Park, Eureka, and Pacific. The North Missouri (Wabash) Railroad opened up Jennings and Ferguson; the West End Narrow Gauge Railroad helped develop Pine Lawn, Normandy, Kinloch, and Florissant.

SEVERING TIES

Ten years after the Civil War, a campaign began to split the city of St. Louis and St. Louis County. The city of St. Louis would become a municipality, and all relations with St. Louis County would be severed. To form two legal entities, the Missouri constitution required a popular vote. The city passed the issue in 1876, but the county didn't. A recount was demanded, and the two were divided.

Without the administration of the city of St. Louis, St. Louis County had to put together a government center. A temporary county seat was established in a hotel at Hanley Road and Olive Street. Soon after, Ralph Clayton offered to donate 100 acres of his farm on the west side of Hanley Road as a permanent location. Clayton had bought the land for about nine dollars an acre in 1821. By 1877, it was worth $300 an acre.

In 1895, entrepreneur Edward Lewis came to St. Louis with a suitcase full of schemes. One of his ideas was to build a planned community, which he named University City because he thought it sounded sophisticated. Lewis didn't stay long—he was always just one step ahead of the law—but he was in the area long enough to found the Lewis Publishing Company, which produced women's magazines that carried more advertising than content. He built a unique octagonal building to house his company and erected lions to guard it. Even though he

Today's county buildings in Clayton are far from temporary. The need for government buildings grew as the county population spread into almost one hundred suburbs.

The Pin-Up Bowl on Delmar Loop East is a new building, constructed in the 1950s art deco style.

abandoned the area, the pattern for out-of-the-ordinary architecture and cultural promotion had been set. Today, the Delmar Loop, which backs up to Washington University, is known for its eclectic mix of art and entertainment.

Farther out in West County, a popular recreational area for fishing, boating, and swimming grew up along the Meramec River in the early 20th century. Resorts, parks, and playgrounds, including Castlewood, Fern Glen, Lincoln Beach, and Meramec Highlands appeared along the bluffs for miles.

After World War II, the GI Bill made new housing available for millions of Americans. Suburbs sprang up across the nation. In St. Louis County, municipalities and school districts struggled to keep up with the rapid growth. Today, the county has more than 91 communities and one million residents, and it continues to grow.

CLAYTON

Clayton may have been a sleepy crossroads in its early history, but since 1960, it's been wide-awake. For 50 years it has grown steadily as a financial, governmental, and legal center. Every week millions of dollars flow through its banks, mortgage companies, and investment firms. Terms like *step-out price, structured notes, leverage,* and *wealth management options* float through the air. Jaguar owners display their classic autos, and jewelry stores promise one-of-a-kind baubles set with perfect gems. Clayton is classy.

Many corporations have facilities in Clayton, including Graybar, Centenne, Brown Shoe, Smurfit-Stone, and Enterprise Rent-a-Car. More are on their way, along with more high-rise office buildings, luxury condos, exclusive shops, and multistar hotels.

Once the St. Louis County government did little more than oversee rural communities and vacant countryside. Now, with its seat in Clayton, it has 21 departments, employs more than 4,300 people, and has an operating budget of $500 million. In the county courts, a variety of cases are adjudicated daily, while the legendary "Clayton lawyer"—synonymous with someone who's brilliant, aggressive, and very expensive—argues the finer points of law. Weaving through ordinances, regulations, assessments, obligations, legal records, and requirements, the county council and county executive have the daunting job of making sense of the patchwork of suburbs and unincorporated areas, while trying to balance the need to go green with the need to promote growth.

Above: George Autenrieth came to Clayton in 1879 and became a civic leader. He built the Autenrieth Hotel, which became a popular place to stay during the 1904 World's Fair. It is seen here in 1914, ten years before the Autenrieth family no longer owned it. Left: Falling Man (Walking Jackman), by St. Louis native Ernest Trova, stands at the corner of Maryland and Brentwood. Trova, the son of a tool designer, was fascinated by the interaction between technology and humanity. He was the impetus behind the establishment of Laumeier Sculpture Park in Sunset Hills, just south of Kirkwood in 1975; he donated 40 sculptures to the initial collection. Trova Woods, a section of the park, honors his work, which has received world-wide recognition.

The St. Louis County Courthouse is seen here in 1945, a few years before the population explosion hit the county. It has been replaced by a constellation of buildings.

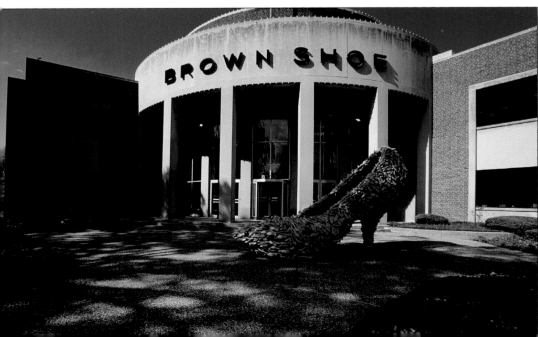

If the Shoe Fits

The giant shoe in front of Brown Shoe Company is made up of tons of shoes, and today Brown Shoe sells its many brands at hundreds of stores around the world. George Warren Brown, who later endowed the School of Social Work at Washington University, began manufacturing shoes in 1878. At the 1904 World's Fair, the company took an interest in a popular cartoon character named Buster Brown (along with his dog Tige) and an icon was born. A patent leather shoe for girls was named for Buster's sister, Mary Jane.

UNIVERSITY CITY

Edward Lewis wanted his University City to be a center of culture and learning. With the Center of Creative Arts (COCA), the St. Louis Philharmonic Orchestra, Craft Alliance, and other craft shops, bookstores, art galleries, and ethnic restaurants, his dream has been realized. Today, University City is multiethnic, multicultural, and wildly diverse in dress and philosophy.

In its early days, U City was a center of Jewish culture. Although there have been changes, that characterization still remains. As middle-class Jews, primarily Reform, moved to West County, Hassidic, Orthodox, and Conservative Jews from a variety of nations—especially Russia—moved in. Congregations today are smaller and more diverse than the ones they replaced. On any Shabbat, Orthodox families can be seen walking west of the Loop to or from services at Agudas Israel or Bais Abraham. Several Jewish schools are in the area as well.

Washington University's influence spreads through U City. Bordering the university, the Parkview residential area is home to many of the university faculty. It has a reputation as an intellectual and literary enclave. The Parkview neighborhood is the one-time home of notable writers Howard Nemerov, Stanley Elkin, John Morris, and William Gass, as well as anthologist Susan Koppelman.

A parade on Delmar in 1941 passes the Tivoli Theater. Opened in 1924, it was an ornate addition to the popular Delmar Loop area of St. Louis.

The marble staircase inside city hall is representative of Lewis's grand plan for the city. It rises to half the height of the lobby, then splits into two staircases that lead to the second floor.

The distinctive octagonal city hall in University City, shown here in the 1940s, was designed in 1902 by Edward G. Lewis for his publishing firm. It was the site of the first convention of the American Women's League in June 1910. The goal of the league, heavily promoted through Lewis's women's magazines, was to provide education for women through his People's University. A year later, a parallel organization called the American Women's Republic was formed. The American Women's League folded in 1912, but the Republic remained.

THE LOOP

More than anyone else, Joe Edwards is responsible for the constant motion of U City's Delmar Loop. The rationale behind the receipt of his long list of awards and honorary degrees can be summed up succinctly: He has both the vision and the follow-through. In 1972, he took a chance on opening a restaurant called Blueberry Hill in the then-seedy 6500 block of Delmar. It almost closed three times in its first two years. Today, some 40 locally owned restaurants have joined his popular Blueberry Hill and there's hardly a time of day or night when the street is deserted.

St. Louis's alternate newspaper, *Riverfront Times*, which is located in the Loop, twice named Edwards "the Best St. Louisan of the Year." He rescued the Tivoli, the city's premier theater for independent and foreign films, and restored it to its 1924 charm. Today's Loop stretches from Kingsland Avenue in U City East into St. Louis to the old Wabash railroad station and includes the Regional Arts Commission, a Joe Edwards-influenced organization; the Pageant, a live-music venue he built and operated; and Pin-Up Bowl, yet another successful Edwards venture.

Every spring, Bradford pear trees burst into bloom along the Delmar Loop. The Loop's many specialty shops and award-winning restaurants attract visitors from all over. The area also plays host to art shows and live music.

The Lure of the Loop

Blueberry Hill anchors the Loop *(above)*. The restaurant's extensive collection of popular culture memorabilia, such as lunch boxes, LP record covers, and Howdy Doody marionettes, caters to the nostalgia of the over-50 crowd, while *Toy Story* and *South Park* tchotchkes please younger patrons. Local bands and perennial favorite Chuck Berry perform regularly in the Duck Room or Elvis Room. Visitors of all ages are also drawn to the Walk of Fame. More than a hundred people associated with St. Louis have been inducted into the St. Louis Walk of Fame, which was also a Joe Edwards project. Bronze stars embedded in the sidewalk on both sides of Delmar Boulevard tell much of the city's history. The oldest member is Pierre Laclede; the youngest is the rapper Nelly. Lou Brock, whose star is shown at right, was a base-stealing Cardinal and is in the Baseball Hall of Fame.

★ BORN JUNE 18, 1939 ★

THE GREATEST BASE STEALER OF HIS ERA, ST. LOUIS CARDINAL LOUIS CLARK BROCK WAS ONLY THE 14TH PLAYER TO HAVE 3,000 HITS. AFTER THREE SEASONS WITH THE CHICAGO CUBS, BROCK JOINED THE CARDINALS IN 1964 AND FUELED THEIR WORLD SERIES VICTORY. DURING HIS 19-YEAR CAREER, THE OUTFIELDER STOLE AN UNPRECEDENTED 938 BASES AND BROKE SEVERAL WORLD SERIES RECORDS, INCLUDING HITTING .391 IN OVER 20 WORLD SERIES GAMES. EXEMPLIFYING THE SPIRIT OF BASEBALL ON AND OFF THE FIELD, BROCK EARNED THE ROBERTO CLEMENTE AND THE JACKIE ROBINSON AWARDS, AMONG MANY OTHERS. A CARDINAL UNTIL HE RETIRED, LOU BROCK ENTERED THE BASEBALL HALL OF FAME ON THE FIRST BALLOT IN 1985.

WEBSTER GROVES

Webster Groves is one of the most gracious St. Louis suburbs; it still has a trace of Victoriana about it. In the late 19th century, Papa could leave stress at the office, take a short train ride from downtown to the Webster station, and walk to his spacious Queen Anne home, where the children would be playing croquet or badminton on the lawn or, in the winter, building snowmen. Many Webster homes were built according to plans taken from *Craftsman Magazine.* They feature an open floor design with built-in bookcases, cabinets, and window seats, which lessens the need for furniture and clutter. For self-improvement, Webster homemakers formed organizations, such as the Monday Club, and became involved in civic betterment and the fight for women's suffrage. In 1911, one of the first Boy Scout troops in the nation was founded in Webster, and a pilot Cub Scout troop followed in 1929.

Founded in 1852 and named for Massachusetts's congressman Daniel Webster, Webster College for Boys gave the city its name. The school disappeared before 1900; it has no connection to today's Webster University. The university was founded in 1915 by the Sisters of Loretto and secularized in 1967. The Opera Theater of St. Louis presents its summer season at the Loretto-Hilton Center on Webster University's campus; the rest of the year, the St. Louis Repertory Theater ("the Rep") takes the stage.

Top: Lockwood Avenue west of Gore is shown here around 1940. Today, the area is called Old Webster and is the site of specialty shops and restaurants. Each year the businesses sponsor a street dance, a jazz festival, and a holiday open house. *Right:* A delightful Queen Anne house, just one of dozens in Webster Groves, gives the area a 19th-century feel.

Family Friendly

Five separate communities along adjacent railroad lines were united in 1896 to make the city of Webster Groves: Webster, Old Orchard, Webster Park, Tuxedo Park, and Selma. Residents lived in houses in countrylike settings within a reasonable distance to downtown St. Louis. Today, the tree-lined streets and single-family homes are still selling points *(above)*; *Family Circle* magazine recently named Webster Groves one of the nation's best cities for families. Additionally, visitors and residents can shop along the streets of Old Webster *(left)* and check out the Old Webster Jazz & Blues Festival that occurs every year.

Kirkwood Station is shown here in the 1930s.

KIRKWOOD

In the 1840s, business leaders hoped St. Louis could be the eastern end of a rail line to the West Coast. It would connect with steamships bound for the Orient, opening trade opportunities. The first step was to get tracks from downtown St. Louis to Jefferson City. In 1850, the newly formed Pacific Railroad Company hired civil engineer James P. Kirkwood to design such a route and oversee its construction. For reasons of his own, Kirkwood did not choose the easiest and cheapest way but the hardest and most expensive: along a ridge between the Meramec and Des Peres rivers. Sections 16 and 17 required hard rock tunneling using mechanical drills, blasting, and brute force with picks, chisels, and shovels. The tunnels were 50 feet deep, with one measuring 630 feet long and the other 440 feet long.

Kirkwood hired about a thousand Irish immigrants to do the work. They lived along the route in thrown-together shanties and were given a whiskey ration to ward off cholera, a preventative that did not work. "Disorderly conduct" was not unusual during the two years it took to complete the job. In 1853, Kirkwood Station welcomed its first train, and the city of Kirkwood became St. Louis's first suburb. Eventually, the line was renamed Missouri-Pacific and became quite profitable under control of the notorious Jay Gould, a railroad developer with a reputation as a "robber baron." In 1982, Mo-Pac merged with Union Pacific. Today, the western-most Barrett's Tunnel is on the grounds of the Museum of Transportation.

Kirkwood's Commuter Hub

In 1947, hopeful riders raced to catch a streetcar *(right)*. Refurbished, Kirkwood Station today *(below)* is frequently the center of activity for the city. It hosts farmers markets, concerts, and art fairs. It is the only suburban Amtrak stop in the St. Louis area. Passengers can board the train there for a short hop downtown or for trips to either coast.

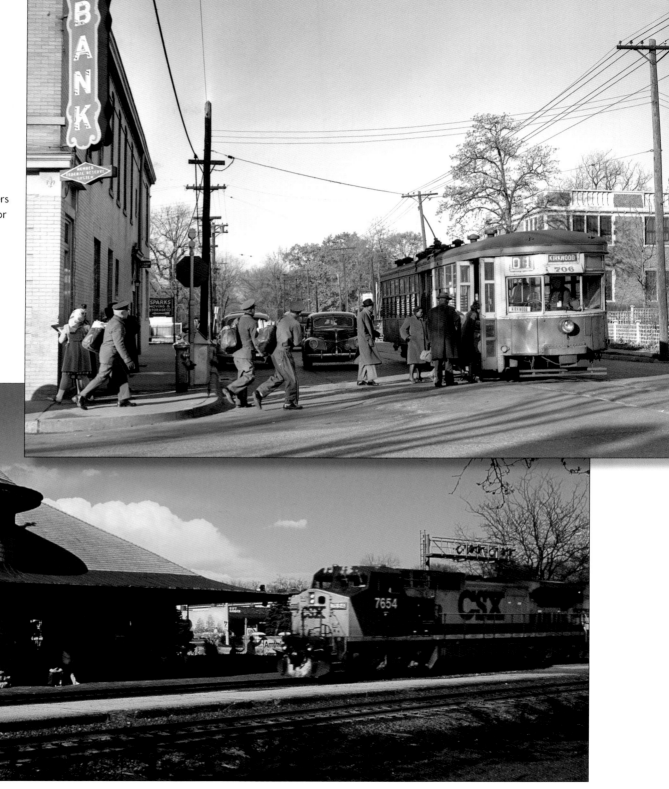

JEFFERSON BARRACKS

As the first permanent military organization west of the Mississippi, Jefferson Barracks was charged with protecting white settlers. Both Missouri territorial governor William Clark and President Thomas Jefferson had advocated the cultivation of good relations with Native Americans, but by the 1820s, many politicians and military leaders saw them as savage killers. Broken treaties, mistrust, looting, and killing on both sides increased as the 19th century progressed. Jefferson Barracks was the first home of the U.S. cavalry, or dragoon regiment as it was called in 1833, when it was organized by Colonel Henry Dodge. Units of the cavalry were sent to forts throughout the West, and the image of their thundering rescues and flying flags would become an indelible part of popular culture.

Jefferson Barracks was the temporary home of the Sauk chief Black Hawk, who was taken prisoner in 1832 after five months of warfare in Illinois and Wisconsin. Two future presidents, Zachary Taylor and Abraham Lincoln, led troops in that war, which ended with the massacre of unarmed members of the Sauk and Fox nations at Bad Axe River in Wisconsin. Jefferson Barracks soldiers also participated in the Mexican War, the Mormon War, the Spanish-American War, the Seminole Wars in Florida, and the two world wars of the 20th century before the barracks closed in 1946.

Top: Jefferson Barracks, shown here between 1861 and 1872, was built to be the first Infantry School of Practice in the United States and a training ground for the western armies. During the Civil War, the barracks served as a military hospital for Union soldiers. By the end of the war, over 18,000 servicemen were treated at Jefferson Barracks Hospital. *Left:* Members of Battery A gather near a cannon around 1899, probably just after the victory in Cuba during the Spanish-American War.

A Place of Honor

A bivouac at Jefferson Barracks served as training grounds for army battalions in 1939 *(above)*. Today, several Revolutionary War soldiers are among the thousands interred at the cemetery on the Jefferson Barracks grounds *(right)*. Graves were originally marked with headboards, some lettered in black stencil. They were replaced by upright engraved marble headstones. In the 1970s, Gold Star Mothers and Fathers of those killed in Korea or Vietnam raised funds for a nonsectarian chapel to honor the dead of all wars: a place of serenity and beauty, a place to find solace and strength. Each Memorial Day, a solemn ceremony is held at the cemetery, and Boy Scouts and Girl Scouts make certain that every grave is honored with a flag.

GRANT'S FARM

Ulysses S. Grant was assigned to Jefferson Barracks after he graduated from West Point in 1843. Fred Dent, whose family owned White Haven southwest of St. Louis, was one of his West Point friends. Through him, Grant met and courted the eldest Dent daughter, Julia, and in 1848, she agreed to marry him. The Grants were sent to several military posts before he resigned from the army in 1854; Grant didn't want to be separated from his growing family. He decided to try to farm the 80 acres on the White Haven property that belonged to Julia. They moved into "Hardscrabble," a house he built himself, in 1856. The next two years were very difficult. Crop yield was poor and prices depressed. There was a bizarre June freeze, typhoid fever and ague visited the family, and debts mounted. In 1860, the Grant family gave up on farming, left White Haven, and moved to Galena, Illinois. A year later, he rejoined the army as colonel of the Seventh District Regiment.

August A. Busch, who preferred farming to brewing, bought Grant's Farm about 50 years after Grant left and stocked it with domestic animals. Some Busch family members still live on the property, as do the famous Clydesdales. About 50 years ago, the Busch family opened a major portion of the grounds—where some thousand animals roam—to the public, free of charge. In 1989, the National Park Service restored nearby White Haven and opened it to the public as well.

Top: White Haven was Julia Dent's childhood home, where she met and was courted by Grant. Shown here in 1979, it is a National Historic Site today. *Bottom:* Today, Grant's Farm is thriving—the area is nothing like the grim, hardscrabble acres in Grant's day.

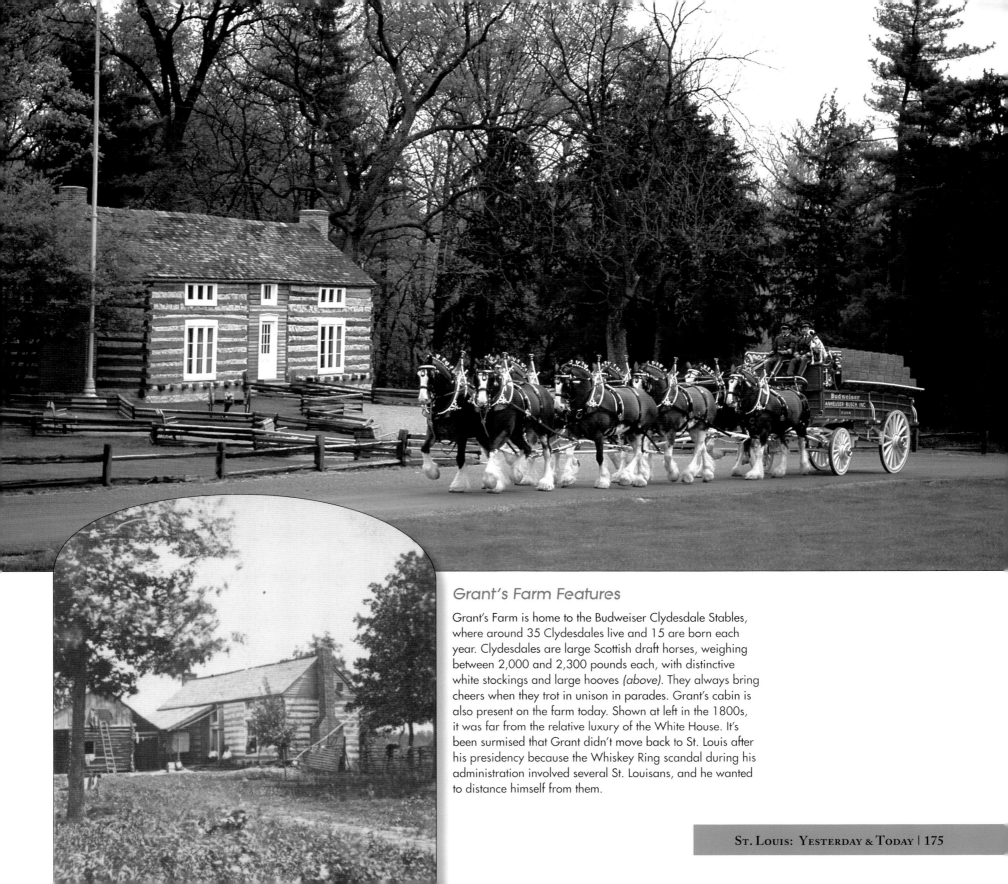

Grant's Farm Features

Grant's Farm is home to the Budweiser Clydesdale Stables, where around 35 Clydesdales live and 15 are born each year. Clydesdales are large Scottish draft horses, weighing between 2,000 and 2,300 pounds each, with distinctive white stockings and large hooves *(above)*. They always bring cheers when they trot in unison in parades. Grant's cabin is also present on the farm today. Shown at left in the 1800s, it was far from the relative luxury of the White House. It's been surmised that Grant didn't move back to St. Louis after his presidency because the Whiskey Ring scandal during his administration involved several St. Louisans, and he wanted to distance himself from them.

UNIVERSITY OF MISSOURI-ST. LOUIS

In 1958, Normandy School District officials wanted to establish a two-year community college, realizing that many of their students could not afford a four-year university. They bought 128 acres of the Bellerive Country Club, which was then moving to West County. To get accreditation, it was necessary for the University of Missouri to supervise the educational program at the school. The terms of accreditation required that at least 100 students attend. As soon as the venture was announced, 140 students applied. With the promise of attendees, the Bellerive clubhouse was renovated with 15 classrooms, two laboratories, a large lecture room, a library, and a cafeteria. The new college opened in September 1960. Enrollment increased to 300 in 1961 and 550 in 1962. It has since been adopted into the University of Missouri system and has grown exponentially.

As enrollment grew, and until new buildings were completed, classes were held in a laundromat at Natural Bridge and Hanley roads and in a church basement across from the campus. Benton Hall opened in 1965; Clark Hall and the library were built next. In 1976, land south of Natural Bridge, the former Marillac College, was acquired. Now a major university with an extensive graduate school, UMSL offers several unique programs such as the World Ecology Center, the Institute for Women in Public Life, and IT Enterprises, an incubator for information technologies.

Above: The 1970s brought a building boom for the campus of UMSL. *Left:* The Marillac (South) campus was dedicated in 1976. Today, the South Campus is the location of UMSL's College of Education, College of Optometry, and College of Nursing.

The Millennium Student Center at UMSL opened in 2000. It houses all student services, as well as amenities such as game rooms, a convenience store, and a bank. It also has a climate-controlled bridge that connects the building to the North Campus Quad.

The Blanche M. Touhill Performing Arts Center was named to honor the former chancellor of UMSL. Its two theaters are designed to allow maximum intimacy between the audience and performers. The Anheuser-Busch Performance Hall has an opera-house feel and presents events such as musicals, classical soloists and ensembles, and popular entertainers. The Lee Theater is a black-box theater—a square, black-walled room—and presents music, theater, and dance performances.

LAMBERT-ST. LOUIS INTERNATIONAL AIRPORT

Albert Bond Lambert worked as an executive with Lambert Pharmaceutical Company, but his great love was aviation. In 1907, long before anyone else saw the possibilities in piloted flight, Lambert formed the Aero Club in St. Louis to promote ballooning and aeroplaning. Orville Wright gave him his first plane ride, and he was the first St. Louisan to get a pilot's license. By 1920, Lambert was leasing a 160-acre cornfield from the owner, Mrs. Mary Jane Weldon; he named it Kinloch Airfield and used it to demonstrate the biplane's speed and agility. In 1923, Lambert expanded his Kinloch Airfield to 316 acres for an international air race that drew Charles Lindbergh as a contestant. Lindbergh decided to stay in St. Louis for a few years, working as an airmail pilot for Robertson Aircraft Company. In 1925, Lambert bought the airfield, now called Lambert Field, from Mrs. Weldon; in 1928, he sold it to the city of St. Louis.

By mid-century, when commercial airlines were rapidly taking passengers away from railroads, Ozark Airlines was established with Lambert Field as its hub. A midsize company, it filled a niche in the Midwest by offering flights to small cities as well as large ones. In 1986, TWA, also with a hub at Lambert Airport, bought the company, and Ozark Airlines disappeared. American Airlines bought TWA in 2001, and so it also disappeared. No airline calls Lambert-St. Louis International Airport home today.

Above: Lambert Field actually used to be a field. Robertson Aircraft, formed by Frank and William Robertson in 1921 as a flying service and airplane manufacturer, became part of American Airways in 1930. *Left:* Minoru Yamasaki's 1956 domed design for Lambert's main terminal was excitingly futuristic. Around 1970, when this photo was taken, the uniforms of flight attendants matched its space-age feel.

Above: In the 1980s, TWA had its main domestic hub at Lambert Airport. Today, the airport has expanded its runways and added an east terminal for Southwest Airlines. *Left:* In 1956, the brand-new terminal received international attention for its striking design.

McDONNELL AND BOEING

MIT-educated engineer James S. McDonnell chose St. Louis as the site to develop an aviation company because of the city's reputation as a "city of flight." Aeronautical engineers from throughout the country were attracted to Curtiss-Wright, Robertson Aircraft, and St. Louis Aircraft during that time, the summer of 1939. McDonnell rented a second-floor office in a building near Lambert Field and began seeking contracts. During World War II, McDonnell Aircraft manufactured seven million pounds of aircraft parts, including tails and engine cowlings for Boeing bombers and Douglas transports. Even before the Korean Conflict, McDonnell was developing jet fighters for the navy—the best known was the Phantom. (McDonnell reputedly had an interest in the supernatural, as well as science, and he chose otherworldly names for his aircraft such as

Phantom, Banshee, Voodoo, and Gargoyle.) Mr. Mac was a hands-on manager and little escaped his attention, even when his corporation grew to be the largest employer in the St. Louis area.

In 1959, NASA awarded McDonnell the contract for Project Mercury, the first U.S. human-controlled spacecraft. Astronaut John Glenn thrilled the world, and especially St. Louisans, when he orbited the earth on February 20, 1962, in a McDonnell space capsule. The successful Gemini program of the mid-60s also used McDonnell-made capsules. In 1967, McDonnell Aircraft merged with Douglas Corporation and became McDonnell-Douglas, with headquarters remaining in St. Louis. In 1997, McDonnell-Douglas merged with the giant Boeing Corporation.

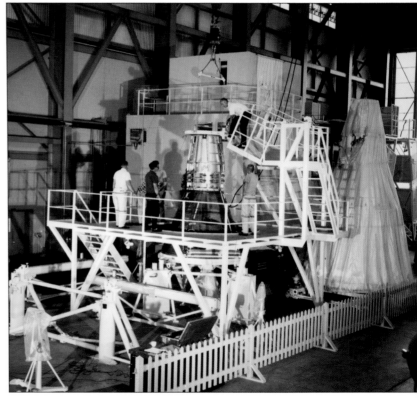

During the early 1960s, McDonnell Aircraft's Phantom II fighter was used by the U.S. Navy, as well as many European air forces (above left). With top speeds of more than twice that of sound, it was one of the most versatile fighters ever built. In 1963, McDonnell engineers worked on the Gemini space capsule (above right), which would take U.S. astronauts into space for two weeks at a time, meeting and docking with orbiting vehicles.

Today, the Boeing offices are located near Lambert Airport. Boeing, manufacturer of commerical and military aircraft and space systems, is headquartered in Chicago.

The 100th F/A-18E/F Super Hornet was delivered to the U.S. Navy in 2002. The supersonic fighter is capable of landing on and taking off from aircraft carriers.

FLORISSANT

The city of St. Ferdinand, which became Florissant in 1939, is the oldest settled area in St. Louis County. The town was probably founded in 1787 or 1788, although at least one settler lived there as early as 1763. Like the town of St. Louis, the settlers were French and the government Spanish between 1768 and 1800, and there was no separation of church and state.

Mother Philippine Duchesne came to Florissant in 1819 to establish a Sacred Heart school for Catholic, Protestant, and Native American girls. As a young nun in France, Sister Duchesne longed to be a missionary to Native Americans. When she was finally allowed to go to the new country of America, she gladly endured poverty, wretched weather, and privations of all sort

for the opportunity to bring Christian education to the frontier. Saint Philippine was canonized in 1988, with many Missouri residents present at the ceremony in Rome.

The cornerstone for the Church of St. Ferdinand, next to the Sacred Heart convent, was laid in February 1821. Two years later, the church was given to the Jesuits, along with a farm that became St. Stanislaus Seminary. In 1958, Joseph Cardinal Ritter moved the boundaries for the St. Ferdinand parish and a new church was built. Preservationists held on to the old church, renaming it the Shrine of St. Ferdinand, and operate it today as a historic site.

St. Ferdinand Shrine in Florissant, shown here in 1936 and today. Its parish was established in 1788.

Rue St. Louis is located in the St. Ferdinand Historic District of Florissant. The area has many historic sites and homes and is a part of Old Town Florrisant.

In the late 19th century, area farmers brought their grain to the gristmill in St. Ferdinand at the intersection of St. Jacques and St. Francois. Later, the building became a post office.

BARN AT LUCERNE AND CHESTERFIELD

The Barn at Lucerne in Ballwin seems strikingly out of place among the suburban-style buildings of West County. Built in 1916 and designed by a Swiss architect, the barn was then the largest dairy facility in the state at 50,000 square feet. The Ganahl family ran it for years. Eventually, St. Louis Dairy took it over and it became part of Sealtest, which later abandoned it. Between 1968 and 1974, the barn suffered a fire and extensive vandalism. It was rescued by historic-minded entrepreneurs who saw the possibilities in such a unique structure. The stalls became shops and offices. A restaurant and tearoom were added.

Chesterfield did not start its life as a suburb, or even a town. It was a constellation of six communities in the mid-19th century, mostly made up of farming families who patronized a general store, blacksmith, sawmill, gristmill, and post office. Today, Chesterfield is the largest suburb/city in St. Louis County, both in area and in population. It has become a corporate center, and the Spirit of St. Louis Airport is lined with executive jets. It's also a regional shopping hub—it's not easy to find a parking place at the sprawling Chesterfield Mall. Chesterfield Commons, the area where Daniel Boone is said to have crossed on his way to his farm in Defiance, Missouri, is now home to numerous big-box stores and franchises.

This general store was built by Edward Burkhardt in the 1890s and was later operated by his son. Its location, just south of Drew Station on Old Olive St. Road, influenced its development as a hotel, saloon, and post office. Today the site is on Chesterfield Airport Road, where it intersects with the north boundary of Baxter Road.

The Barn in Ballwin houses a variety of shops, offices, and watering holes; within the complex are three restaurants, a music venue, a private school, and a fitness center. The spires, beams, and unique look make it stand out from its surroundings.

With people drawn to its corporate and shopping centers, Chesterfield is one of the fastest-growing suburbs in St. Louis County.

MERAMEC RIVER RESORTS

As soon as railroads reached the Meramec, St. Louisans turned the river into a summertime resort. Land was cheap, and summer cabins, from the crude to the elaborate, popped up along the bluffs. Swanky resorts drew city folk looking for relief from the heat. Times Beach, Lincoln Beach, the Meramec Highlands, and Castlewood were popular destinations. During Prohibition, the heavily wooded area was a perfect hideaway for bootleggers and speakeasies. Frequent floods of the Meramec, coupled with the loss of several resorts to fire, made the area less attractive for vacationing. St. Louisans also left the area in the 1950s mainly because the interstate highway system opened up more options.

In the fall of 1982, Times Beach was suddenly in the news. Years earlier, the towns' dusty streets had been coated with oil because the administration couldn't afford paving. Many of the 1,200 residents noticed that birds and animals died shortly afterward, but the County Health Department did not follow up. Then the EPA discovered that the oil, and therefore the ground, was contaminated with dioxin. Compounding the situation was a December flood of the Meramec, spreading dioxin and other poisonous pollutants into businesses and homes. The entire town was cordoned off and eventually bought out. In 1996 and 1997, 265,000 tons of contaminated soil were removed and incinerated. The State of Missouri turned the site into Route 66 State Park.

Lincoln Beach was a popular place during its heyday in the 1930s.

Route 66 State Park

Route 66 was designated a national highway in 1926, and it stretched from Chicago to Los Angeles. It entered Missouri at St. Louis and traveled diagonally to Joplin, generally following the course of today's I-44. Known as "the Mother Road," Route 66 became part of American pop culture with songs, TV shows, kitschy attractions, and lots of memorabilia. The visitor center at the Route 66 State Park, which has much of that memorabilia, is the former Steiny's Inn, a favorite stop in the 1940s and 1950s. The park offers plenty of scenic spots to bike, walk, watch birds, or just study nature.

Index